P9-DHQ-939

ACHIEVING THE ULTIMATE IMAGE

Ernst Wildi

AMHERST MEDIA, INC. ■ BUFFALO, NEW YORK

Copyright © 1998 by Ernst Wildi

All rights reserved.

Published by:
Amherst Media, Inc.
P.O. Box 586
Buffalo, NY 14226
Fax: 716-874-4508

Publisher: Craig Alesse
Senior Editor/Project Manager: Richard Lynch
Associate Editor: Frances J. Hagen

Photos by: Ernst Wildi

ISBN: 0-936262-62-1
Library of Congress Catalog Card Number: 97-077173

Printed in the United States of America
10 9 8 7 6 5 4 3 2 1

No part of this publication may be reproduced, stored, or transmitted in any form or by any means, electronic, mechanical, photocopied, recorded, or otherwise, without prior written consent from the publisher.

Notice of disclaimer: The information contained in this book is based on the author's experience and opinions. The author and publisher will not be held liable for the use or misuse of the information in this book.

Table of Contents

Chapter Six

Lenses for Creating the Ultimate Sharpness 27

Chapter Seven

Effective Use of Lenses & Lens Controls 35

Chapter Eight

Achieving the Ultimate Exposure 48

Introduction

To achieve the ultimate image is to create an image that is technically perfect and visually inspiring. If you do photography as a hobby, achieving this goal may mean nothing more than creating an image that pleases you — the creator of the image. Naturally your photographic hobby becomes more rewarding if the images also bring enjoyment to others. It should convey to your friends, family members, or members of a camera club that you know what to do with a roll of film in the camera.

For the professional, it is important that the image pleases the client. It needs to convey the message that the client is trying to get across, such as in an advertisement. It can convince the client that you are the professional that should be considered for future assignments. Such an image must have visual impact, mainly determined by your artistic sense for design and color. The image must also be free from any technical faults that may distract from the impact or enjoyment of the image.

This book covers the points that are important for creating such an image with any camera. It does so in a simple fashion, without going into details about camera design, the features and operation of specific cameras, lenses and accessories. You can find that information in your instruction manual. I also assume that you know and understand the basics of photography, films and use of cameras. I limit my text to how this knowledge is applied for creating good looking, exciting photographs.

The book will inspire you to look for new, exciting picture ideas and to record ordinary subjects in a different way, thus, achieving the ultimate image technically as well as visually.

I have used Hasselblad equipment exclusively for many years and most of the images in the book are made with Hasselblad. Because of this, the illustrations show Hasselblad items, but everything in the book also applies to 35mm photography.

"...create an image that is technically perfect and visually inspiring."

CHAPTER ONE

Film or No Film

Until recently, photography always meant recording images on transparency or negative film, then projecting the slides on a projection screen or producing black and white or color prints from the negatives in the darkroom.

Most special effects, such as changes in color, multiple exposures, and blurred motion, had to be created when recording the image.

Today, we have the second possibility of recording the images electronically, viewing them on a computer or TV screen, or producing prints without film, photographic paper and without a darkroom. Unlimited special effects can be electronically added later. You can save on film and processing costs while helping the environment, since there are no chemicals involved.

So a first question for the newcomer is: "Which way should I go, film or digital?" For a working photographer, the questions is: "Should I change to electronic imaging or add electronic imaging to my present photographic involvement?" Although electronic imaging is fairly new, there is already an avalanche of equipment available both for serious professional work as well as for the point & shoot approach.

The Point & Shoot Approach

There is a wide range of digital cameras that are very much like point & shoot cameras for films. They look similar, are about the same size, and weigh about the same: between five and twelve ounces. The features on these cameras are very similar — usually providing automatic exposure, automatic focusing or fixed focus, some with zoom lenses, some with flash.

On some models, the image is viewed through an optical finder. On others, the image is displayed on an LCD panel so you can see what the final image will look like. A certain number of images can be stored in memory in the camera. Some cameras offer the opportunity to store more images on PC cards.

The images can later be viewed on the computer screen. You may have the possibility of retouching or manipulating the images with imaging software and make prints yourself, or have them made at a digital workstation.

While we are not talking about serious photography here, you may very well want to add such a digital point & shoot camera for your personal work, for family snapshots, or for just having fun.

"Unlimited special effects can be electronically added later."

If you plan to add such a digital point & shoot camera, look at the various models. Try them to see which one is most enjoyable in actual use. Look at some of the specifications — especially how many images can be stored, how fast the camera cycles, whether the images can be downloaded into your computer, and the resolution capability which determines the image quality.

Digital Imaging for Serious Work

For photojournalists and some professional photographers in the commercial and fashion photography field, electronic imaging is nothing new. High quality digital cameras have been available for a few years; new models are added constantly. Many of them are built around an established 35mm camera. Camera operation and the actual recording of the image is done in the same fashion as with film.

Most of the information in this book (such as the use of lenses, lens controls, close-up photography, use of flash, compositions) applies also to electronic imaging with these cameras. The size of the digital image is usually smaller than a 35mm frame, so you must realize that the standard lens becomes a telephoto. A lens with a focal length somewhere around 25mm will cover the same area as the standard for 35mm. You will undoubtedly have a great need for wide angles and extreme wide angle lenses. Image quality varies on these cameras, so check the specifications.

The images are stored digitally and can be downloaded into a computer. Image processing, data transmission, and printing are accomplished within a very short time. This is an advantage in advertising photography. An ad with images can be completed and ready for printing within two to three hours from the moment the image is made in the camera. The usually tight deadlines for newspapers and magazines are a major reason why photojournalism has moved to electronic imaging. Another is the possibility of transmitting these digital images immediately to other places around the globe.

When considering digital equipment for your work, you must determine beforehand what it will be used for and especially what size prints you need for that application. Then check the specifications, or even better, actually try it, use it in a typical application, and make prints in the size you need. Basically, it is the same recommendation that is made for film photography — selecting a certain film format and/or piece of equipment for a specific application. You may not want to use 35 mm if you need gigantic enlargements, but shoot the original in the medium or large format that provides the necessary sharpness for the blow-up.

Digital Imaging in the Medium and Large Format

Medium and large format photographers have been able to produce images electronically for some time by simply attaching a special electronic imaging back to existing cameras. There is no need to buy a new camera or camera system. You use the same camera, lenses and accessories that you use for film.

You must, however, study the specifications for the digital back. Some are only usable with specific camera models, even among those made by the same company. You may need a motordriven camera. You may have to be directly connected to the computer, limiting the photographic work to the studio. Others can be taken into the field, recording the images on a PC

"...actual recording of the image is done in the same fashion as with film."

card. You must also check whether the image is scanned or recorded instantly in all colors. The latter will allow photography of moving subjects and the use of electronic flash. Also check the size of the frame. Most are more of the size of a 35mm than medium format. If this is the case, standard lenses record like telephotos. To record the standard frame, the lens must have a wide angle focal length.

Applications for Digital Imaging

Recording images electronically is an exciting addition to film photography that must be taken seriously, at least by the professional photographer. As a serious professional, keep up to date, study the possibilities in electronic imaging, see what is possible and what is happening.

Even if you continue to record your images on film, as you probably will, adapting to some of these new possibilities will keep you ahead of the competition. Digital imaging is a logical consideration for any type of photography where Polaroids may have been used before — in the real estate and insurance fields, for example.

While electronic imaging has advantages in some fields and applications, I consider it an addition, not a replacement, for photography with film. Unless you see a specific advantage in your work, I suggest continuing using film, especially if image quality is a main concern as it is to most photographers.

If your main interest is in retouching or manipulating the image, or in filing and transmitting images, keep in mind that the original need not be digital. Any image on film can be changed into digital: you can make digital prints or transparencies yourself from the original film images or have them done at a digital workstation. For most professional photographers, this is the most logical solution.

Since film is likely to remain the choice for most serious photography, electronic imaging and digital equipment are not discussed in further detail in the following chapters. However, since the approaches and techniques for recording the image are the same or similar in both media, most of the information in the book should be helpful whether you record the image on film or electronically.

"...I consider it an addition, not a replacement..."

CHAPTER TWO

Films for the Ultimate Image Quality

Today, as in the past, image quality varies with the sensitivity of the films. Films of lower sensitivity produce sharper images than those with higher ISO numbers. For producing the ultimate image sharpness in any film format, consider films with ISO 50 to 100. However, the grain structure and the resolution of practically all the films we have today are far superior to those films we had just five years ago.

This superb definition allows us to record details and make gigantic enlargements unimaginable in the past. It also means that you should not hesitate to use faster films — 400 ISO or higher if it helps you produce the desired results for your photographic approach. The sharpness of ISO 400 films today is what ISO 100 was five years ago.

Switching to a higher ISO film allows you to use a smaller aperture for greater depth of field, a shorter shutter speed to decrease the danger of camera or subject movement, to do hand-held photography, or to work with a smaller flash unit. An image taken with ISO 400 film at $f/8$ may very well be visibly more effective due to the greater depth of field than one made at $f/4$ on ISO 100. If hand-held photography is necessary or desirable, I prefer to use the shorter 1/125 sec. shutter speed with ISO 400 over 1/30 sec. with ISO 100.

Transparency films are generally recognized as sharper than color negative emulsions. Prints made directly from transparencies (especially in the medium format) also have the ultimate sharpness and contrast, but they are only made in special professional labs and at high costs, or in your own darkroom. Amateur labs do not make such prints or only by making first a negative (internegative) from the transparency. This process thus eliminates or reduces the advantages of shooting the original on transparency film. If you need color prints, it is best to use color negative emulsions, with a low ISO, if sharpness is a main concern.

Evaluating the Final Image

The sharpness of a projected transparency is affected by the brightness and quality of the projector and its projection lens. If you want to show

"…image quality varies with the sensitivity of the films."

your slides with the corner-to-corner sharpness recorded in the camera, evaluate the sharpness features of the projector carefully. Consider a higher quality projection lens than the one that comes with the projector.

When you tilt a projector to move the image on the screen up or down, maintaining sharpness from top to bottom is always a problem. Perspective control built into a projector will eliminate this problem, but it is a feature that is hard to find. Projectors are readily available for 35mm, for the 6x6 and 6x4.5 medium format, and even for 6x7.

The sharpness, contrast and overall quality of a black and white and color print is greatly dependent on the film development, the quality of the printing equipment, and the paper and paper development.

For ultimate sharpness in the final image, the quality of the printing equipment and materials must match the quality of the camera and lens. A larger film format is likely to call for better quality in the rest of the photographic equipment.

If a projected transparency or a print does not have the expected quality, evaluate first the negative or original transparency under a good magnifying glass. Its magnification should be 8x or better 10x. A 3x or 4x loupe is not sufficient for critical work.

Examine the negative or transparency carefully. Try to determine whether the deficiency of the quality that you noticed on the screen or print is visible on the original. This will likely reveal at what stage in the image creating process the problem is located.

Even if there is no sharpness problem with the final image, I recommend that you examine all your negatives or transparencies under a 8x or 10x magnifier.

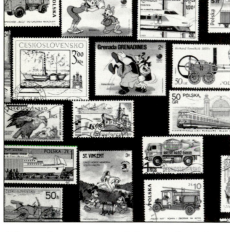

The enlarging capability with today's films is illustrated by the 10x enlargement of the postage stamps. The original was made in the 6x6cm format on Kodak T-Max 100 ASA film. The original is pictured above, the enlargement is shown at the right.

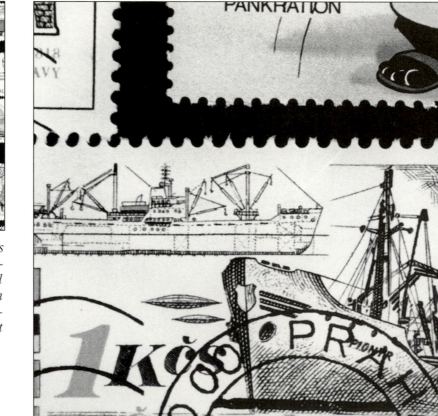

You will be able to see more in this examination than you will ever see on the final image. For example, the difference in sharpness within the depth of field range and the difference in sharpness between ISO 100 and ISO 400 film. This constant check of your images will make you a very critical photographer.

The magnifier does not need to be of a high optical quality, since you basically only view the center of the magnified image. However, a high quality type that may cost 5 or even 10 times more makes such evaluation more enjoyable and more critical.

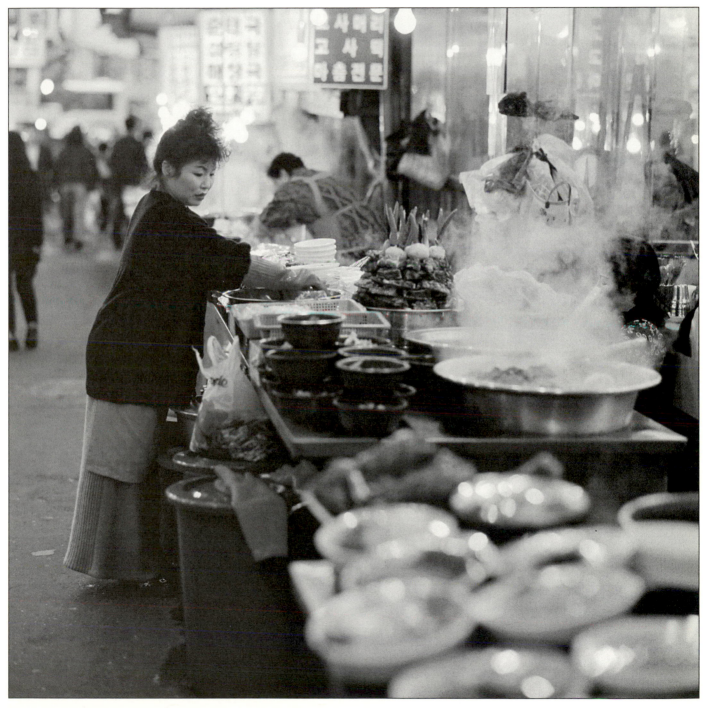

Higher sensitivity films, such as ISO 400, have excellent sharpness without any objectionable or visible grain, especially in the larger medium format. Such films allow hand-held photography in low light situations as at this marketplace in Korea.

CHAPTER THREE

Selecting the Film Format

"...image sharpness is dependent on the size of the image on the film."

Regardless of the type of film in the camera, image sharpness is dependent on the size of the image on the film. On a larger negative or transparency, the subject is recorded proportionally larger. The subject is spread over a larger area, revealing more details or revealing them in a sharper fashion. In principle then, a larger image format will produce a sharper image (assuming that everything else is equal). There are four major photographic formats: large format (4x5in. and larger), the various medium formats, 35mm, and the new APS (Advanced Photo System).

The Large Format

4x5in. and larger is basically a professional format. It has been and is still used, however, by many amateur photographers in the fine art field, especially for black and white work.

Its importance, however, has been diminished because of the high quality of today's black and white and color films. The smaller film formats allow gigantic blow-ups that come close to the 4x5in. quality. The negatives can also be produced in a smaller, more compact camera that even allows hand-held work. The main advantage of working with large format view cameras today is in the cameras' shift and tilt capability.

The Medium Formats

Unlike 35mm, where all cameras produce the same 24x36mm image size, medium format cameras are made for different image sizes. Some cameras provide a choice of two or three sizes with interchangeable magazines.

The medium format is about as old as photography. Daguerreotype plates were usually in sizes between 2 and 4 inches. The folding cameras were made for the medium format (6x9cm) and the box brownies were made for the 120 or 620 roll film. The medium format became established for serious photography with the introduction of the Twin lens reflex cameras producing 6x6cm square images.

The 2¼ Square Format

The 2¼ square (6x6cm) format is still the most popular all over the world. The image area is more than 3½ times larger than 35mm. The square images

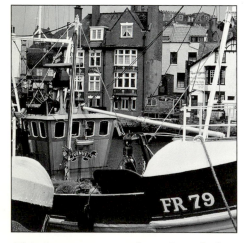

This image was made with a 6x6cm (2¼ square) medium format camera. Compare this photo with those found on page 16.

can be produced without the need for turning a camera This is a wonderful advantage while shooting, working from a tripod, or working with a portable flash unit attached to the camera. If properly composed, square images can be changed into verticals or horizontals later without losing sharpness. We are not cropping, just changing the shape of the image. On some square format cameras, you can also produce rectangular images in the 6x4.5cm format with a different magazine or by inserting a mask.

The 6x4.5cm Format

Some medium format cameras are specifically made for the 6x4.5cm format which has an image area about 2.6x larger than 35mm. The long side of the negative is 56mm, 1.6x longer than the 36mm long side of 35mm. Subjects on 6x4.5 (or 6x6cm) are therefore about 1.6x larger. Since the long sides of 2¼ square and 6x4.5cm images are identical, image sharpness is equal provided everything else is equal. 2¼ square and 6x4.5cm cameras are compact and easy to use on location for hand-held photography.

The 6x7cm Format

A third popular medium format is 6x7cm, with the long side of the negative or transparency 1cm longer than the 2¼ square or 6x4.5cm format; 1.9x longer than 35mm. Theoretically, this format should produce sharper images, but the difference in negative size seem to be too small to make such a difference noticeable. The slightly larger image, however, can increase size and weight of the camera considerably. This must be considered in a medium format camera. It determines whether photography is a pleasure or a burden and whether the camera becomes strictly a studio type or an equally great tool for hand-held location photography. This flexibility is what a medium format camera is suppose to produce.

6x7cm, however, is selected often, especially for studio work, because of the rectangular shape of the image. Also, horizontals and verticals may be obtained by turning the film magazine, not the entire camera, and because of the camera shape which may be more like a 35mm type.

Interchangeable Film Magazines

The larger image size is a major reason for selecting the medium format. A second, and for many photographers equally important, is the camera design with interchangeable film magazines. With the film in a separate film magazine, which is removable at any time, you can switch from one type of film to another — even in the middle of a roll — without wasting or fogging the film. You can switch from black and white to color, from low speed to high speed film, or from 120 to 220 or 70mm long roll films.

On most cameras, you can also attach a magazine for Polaroid film. Shooting a Polaroid allows checking the camera operation or the flash sync at any time. It also allows for complete image evaluation — especially advantageous when using slow shutter speeds to blur action, producing double exposures, or other effects that cannot be seen on the focusing screen.

Backs for electronic imaging can also be added to some cameras. While it is at present a costly proposition (intended only for the professional who needs this approach to satisfy a client), it is something you may want to keep in the back of your mind. It will allow you to go into electronic imaging without investing in a completely new and different camera system.

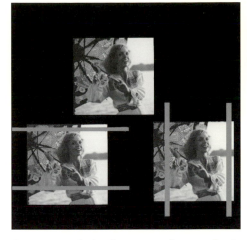

Images made in the square format don't have to be presented as squares. Many images can be changed effectively into horizontals or verticals afterwards. The images can also be composed as verticals or horizontals on the square focusing screen.

"The larger image size is a major reason for selecting the medium format."

Other Medium Formats

Other image sizes that belong to the medium format field because they are produced on 120 or 220 roll film are 6x8cm, 6x9cm and the panoramic shapes 6x12 or 6x17cm.

35mm

35mm cameras produce excellent image sharpness for amateur and professional work on today's high resolution films. So good, in fact, that some photographers and photographic educators feel that there is no need anymore to move up to a larger format, not even the medium format sizes.

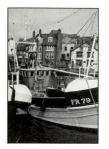

This image was taken with the 35mm format camera. Compare this to the photo below and the one on page 14.

35mm images today are much sharper than a few years ago. They can be enlarged to greater sizes without grain or unsharpness becoming visible or objectionable. Since identical films are used in the medium format, the same quality difference between 35mm and the larger formats still exists today. I feel that the best reason for moving from 35mm to the medium format is exactly the superb sharpness of the films today. While 35mm images look beautiful, only a larger format can really convey the quality that is possible on these films. It is exciting to view medium format negatives or transparencies under a 10x magnifying glass. You can really experience what image sharpness means today.

35mm is an excellent choice for many professional applications and definitely for amateur photographers. The choice of camera is unlimited; from fully automatic, compact and lightweight models to the very sophisticated type with a wide choice of lenses and accessories. While some of the latter camera bodies with built-in motor may weigh as much as some of the compact medium format models, lenses will be more compact and weigh less. This will be appreciated by the nature, wildlife or sport photographers working with long telephotos. The 35mm format offers the fastest lenses available. In most focal lengths, such lenses may be one or two stops faster than equivalent focal lengths in the medium format. 35mm also gives you the widest choice of films which are available worldwide.

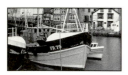

This image was taken with the Advanced Photo System or APS. Compare this to the photo above and the one on page 14.

The Advanced Photo System

Cameras made for the APS system produce images on film loaded in a special cassette designed for completely automatic loading. All images on the film are the same size (16.7x30.2mm) but they can be composed and later printed in three different formats: Classic (C) using the full 16.7x30.2mm image area in the classic 2:3 ratio; HDTV (H) with a 9:16 ratio; or Panoramic (P) with a 1:3 ratio.

While all images are smaller than 35mm, image sharpness has been found to be excellent — more than satisfactory for amateur enlargement. The compact camera design is one of the benefits of the APS format. Its main advantages are not in the photographic possibilities, but in the storing and printing convenience. These points are of course less important to us, the serious photographers, than the versatility and possibilities of creating interesting images of the highest quality. Consequently, this new format should not be considered at present for serious photography. The tools for creating such images are limited or non-existent. You may, however, consider such a camera for your personal work.

CHAPTER FOUR

Camera Features

Cameras are available in a wide variety of styles and types. You should have no problem finding one in your price range that has the essentials for producing your type of images in the best and easiest way. For serious work, you probably want to consider a single lens reflex type where you can evaluate the image carefully on the focusing screen.

Shutters

There is also a choice of shutter: focal plane type built in the camera or one in the lens. For most purposes, one is as good as the other. A lens shutter, however, will allow you to shoot with electronic flash at all shutter speeds — especially helpful when using flash outdoors in bright daylight. Many 35mm cameras synchronize up to 1/250 sec or even 1/300 sec which is short enough for most applications.

Focal plane shutters in medium format cameras are more limited, usually providing flash sync only up to 1/60 sec, or 1/90 sec at best. You must therefore select the shutter type more carefully in the medium format. The shutter speeds, either in the camera or the lens, can be controlled mechanically or electronically. The latter is more reliable and accurate in cold weather. One must realize, however, that the actual shutter operation is always mechanical, and good mechanical shutters can be practically as accurate as electronic types — but they require more attention for service.

Viewfinders

For achieving the ultimate image sharpness, the camera's viewfinder must be carefully evaluated. Regardless of the type of finder, you must be able to see the focusing screen on an SLR type with utmost clarity. When you look through a camera viewfinder, you no longer look at the actual focusing screen but at an image of the screen, which is at a specific distance — usually around 2 to 6 feet. Your instruction book may not give you this information, so check with the manufacturer of the camera.

It is important to know this as your eyes must be capable of focusing at this distance (this is often not the case, especially with older photographers). Fortunately, on most cameras today, eyepieces are adjustable or interchangeable so the eyepiece correction can be matched to your personal

"You should have no problem finding one in your price range..."

17

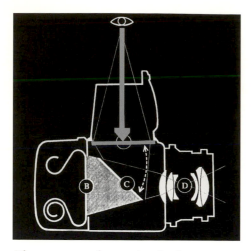

The purpose of any viewfinder, on any 35mm or medium format SLR camera, is to provide a sharp, magnified image of the focusing screen.

eyesight. Investigate this point carefully when you purchase the camera. The correction you may need has no direct relationship to the eyeglass prescriptions, as the two are made for different distances.

Try the different eyepieces or obtain more information from the camera manufacturers. Do not compromise on this point. Don't be satisfied until you have a solution that gives you the sharpest possible view. Most cameras today also have what is called a high eyepoint eyepiece. Such an eyepiece should allow you to view and focus with or without eyeglasses and always see the entire finder field.

Now you have the choice of leaving the eyeglasses on or removing them when taking a photograph. This must be your choice. While I realize that removing glasses is a nuisance (especially when you need them for reading the figures on the camera and lenses), I suggest this approach for hand-held photography. For camera steadiness, any camera viewfinder must be firmly pressed against the eye and forehead. You have a firmer support pressing it directly against the eye instead of the eyeglasses. I make removing the eyeglasses more convenient by hanging the glasses on a chain so they can be dropped easily. If you decide on viewing with glasses, the eyepiece correction must be made accordingly. Astigmatism is seldom a factor in viewing through a camera viewfinder.

The image you see in the viewfinder is optically magnified. Eyepiece magnification should be considered, especially on SLR types. A higher magnification will likely help you to focus faster and more accurately.

Focusing Screens

Focusing screens on SLR cameras come in plain ground-glass, with split image rangefinder or microprism, or a combination of the two. This must be your personal choice. You must consider seriously the brightness and sharpness of the image.

Brighter screens make composition easier, especially when photographing in low light levels, but do not necessarily make focusing faster or more accurate. For this, you need a sharp looking image on the screen. Superb sharpness has been accomplished on some of the modern screens where the ground-glass surface is practically invisible. It is almost like a microprism over the entire surface with the image visibly "jumping in and out of focus."

Automatic focusing works beautifully in most cameras and may actually produce sharper results for photographers with a viewing problem. Naturally, we the photographers must always decide on what part of the subject to focus. We must be able to lock the focus and have the option for manual focusing if we do anything more serious than snapshooting.

On all SLR cameras, the mirror swings up and down every time we take a picture. There is always the possibility that such a mirror does not go back to the same exact position after thousands of exposures. If so, focusing is no longer correct. Have the mirror alignment checked once in a while by an authorized service station.

Motordriven Film Advance

Motordriven film advance is an expected feature built into today's better 35mm cameras. Motordrives are also a part of many medium format cameras — if not built into the camera then available as an accessory motor winder.

"Have the mirror alignment checked once in a while..."

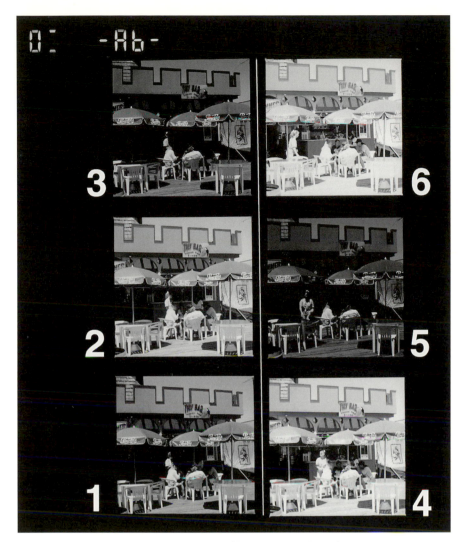

A motordrive in a camera may also offer the possibility of automatic exposure bracketing, here done in ⅔ f-stops.

For most photographers, the motordrive is nothing more than a convenience, eliminating the need to advance the film manually.

In some fields of photography (sports, for example), the main benefit is fast sequence shooting (some 35mm's are able to shoot several images per second). Such sequence photography offers greater possibility of capturing an event or action at the most effective moment, naturally at the expense of using up a lot of film. In the medium format, the speed of shooting is reduced down to about one image per second.

There are other benefits to a motordrive. Sequences of images can be made without the danger of moving a mounted camera between images. This can be especially helpful in close-up work, in scientific photography, and in copying.

The main benefit of the motordrive for most photographers is simply that you can keep your eye constantly in the viewfinder. Therefore, you maintain constant contact with your subject, just pressing the release at the perfect moment and not missing great pictures by not being ready. Fashion photographers will point this out as their main reason for using motordriven cameras.

"...you can keep your eye constantly in the viewfinder."

For the same reason, the motordrive can help the portrait photographer — especially when photographing babies and children who constantly change position and expression. In this and other applications, the possibility of operating some motordriven cameras from a distance can be an additional benefit. You need not stand behind the camera. You can be next to the baby or child, making it easier to obtain a precious expression, which is so important in baby and child photography.

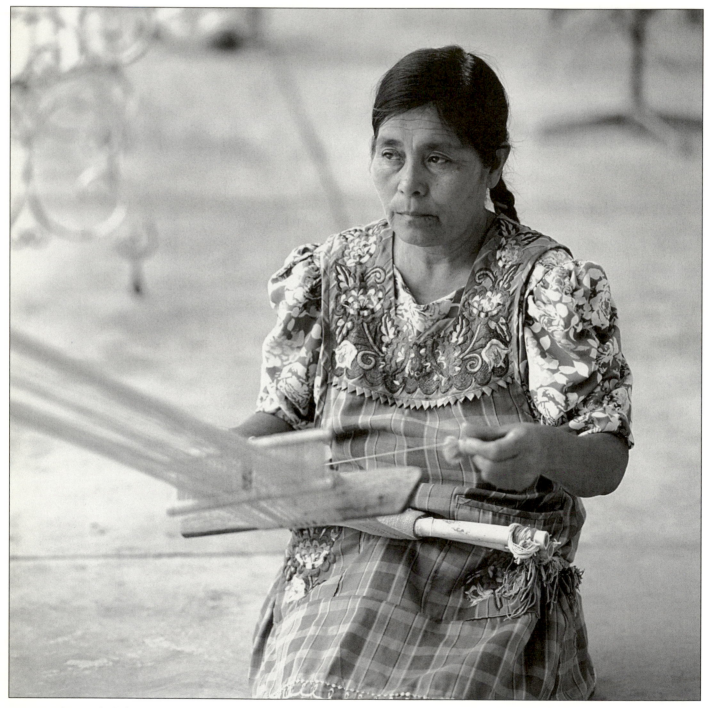

A motordrive is helpful when photographing people, allowing you to keep your eye in the viewfinder and maintain constant contact with the subject. This photo was taken in Mexico.

In all these applications, you do not need a camera that shoots several frames per second: about one picture per second is just right. That is about as long as it takes for a person to turn the head or body, to go from a serious to a happy expression or vice versa, or for a model to fall into a new pose.

The motordrive is equally helpful when photographing people anywhere in the world — whether candidly or when they know they are being photographed. A motordriven camera also encourages hand-held photography. Whether this is good or bad depends on the field of photography or the photographer's shooting habits. Some commercial illustrators who were pretty much tied to tripod work found new freedom, new enjoyment, and new creative opportunities working with a hand-held 35mm or medium format camera. These positives can easily outweigh the negative part of the motordrive — the additional weight and bulk of the equipment.

A motordriven 35mm or medium format camera may also provide automatic exposure bracketing which is helpful when you must shoot fast — in sports, for example. In most of my work, using a precise built-in spot metering system, I seldom find a need for bracketing and if I do, I prefer to do it manually. The main reason: I like to know exactly when the exposure is made when I photograph people. Also, my bracketing value changes from one situation to the other. Automatic bracketing, however, can be helpful in many situations when using a less precise metering system, and especially if one does not have a complete understanding of exposure.

A Word about Batteries

Motordrives, like other camera functions, need batteries. Usually a specific type must be used so you have no choice. When standard A, AA, or AAA types are called for, you usually have a choice of the standard Alkaline, Lithium or rechargeable type. While standard Alkaline types serve the purpose, the more expensive Lithium types last longer, give more exposures, and are more reliable in cold temperatures. It pays to spend the additional money. Always carry spare batteries for the motordrive and all the other camera functions.

"A motordriven camera also encourages hand-held photography."

Chapter Five

Camera Operation for Image Quality & Effect

"...use the approach that will produce the desired results..."

For maximum image sharpness, a camera must be perfectly motionless during the time the shutter is open and the exposure is made. Contrary to some photographers' belief, achieving the ultimate image sharpness does not necessarily require a tripod.

With 35mm, APS and even medium format cameras, hand-held photography can create images equal in sharpness to those created using a tripod. Use your judgment: use the approach that will produce the desired results in the most effective way without taking away the enjoyment of your photography.

The hand-held approach is suggested not only when you have to work fast to capture people candidly, but also to encourage photographing from different camera angles. It is time-consuming to set up a tripod and change tripod height. It is even more time-consuming to move the tripod around while you are investigating different camera angles.

Some tripods also make it difficult to get low camera angles. As a result, tripod photographers tend to photograph everything from the same, most convenient, tripod height. If you want or need to use a tripod, I suggest that you first investigate all the possible angles and use of lenses before placing the camera on the tripod.

Move around the subject with a hand-held camera, view the scene from different angles and distances or through different lenses, look at the subject from low and high camera angles. Don't set up the tripod until you have thoroughly exhausted all possibilities and found the most effective camera position.

Naturally there is nothing wrong with photographing the subject in several different ways so you can determine later which view makes the most effective image.

The main drawback for hand-held photography is that it limits the choice of shutter speed and thus the choice of aperture and depth of field. Hand-held photography also makes you more likely to select films of a higher sensitivity where the slower, somewhat sharper films could have been used with a tripod.

Successful Hand-held Photography

Cameras can be held in many ways. Try different methods until you find one that you feel provides the greatest steadiness. You may also find that different lenses call for different approaches. For example, a camera equipped with a longer telephoto is better held differently than when used with a shorter lens.

However you hold the camera, you need a firm foundation. Start by standing with your feet apart. Press your elbows into your body for additional support.

To hold something steady, you need two forces opposing each other: one pushing one way, the other pressing in the opposite direction. This condition is obtained when the hands press the camera firmly against the eye while the forehead pushes in the opposite direction. A firm contact between the eye and the camera eyepiece thus becomes the main determining factor for camera steadiness.

From this point of view, it is recommended to view without eyeglasses, placing the necessary eyepiece correction into the camera viewfinder. This is possible in one way or another on most cameras today.

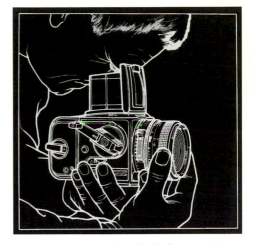

Contrary to popular belief, a medium format camera is not limited to tripod work. A compact camera makes an excellent and successful tool for hand-held operation.

Effective Use of a Tripod

The use of a tripod is recommended when using longer lenses and/or longer shutter speeds. For example, when photographing subjects or close-ups where the point of focus must be clearly established when evaluating the image on the focusing screen; in portrait or fashion photography where directing the people is most important; when the composition must be carefully evaluated on the focusing screen; or when sequences of identical images must be produced.

Most photographers' approach to tripod photography means releasing the camera with a cable release while standing away from the tripod. This is the recommended or necessary approach when shutter speeds are longer than ½ or 1 second.

At shorter shutter speeds, you can reduce or eliminate the danger of camera motion by doing just the opposite. Place your hands on top of the tripod or camera with your eye pressed against the viewfinder as you do for hand-held photography. Lay your own weight on top of the tripod, pressing tripod and camera to the ground.

You can use a cable release, however you really do not need it for this approach where the tripod acts more like a supplementary support than the sole means of supporting and steadying the camera.

This method of tripod photography allows you to obtain good steadiness, even with a lightweight tripod and longer lenses, something you will appreciate when travelling.

Mirror Lock up

Whenever you work from a tripod, camera, or copying stand with any SLR camera, be sure to lock up the mirror so camera motions that might produce vibrations (such as the mirror lift up) are performed before the exposure is made.

While this so-called pre-releasing is really necessary only at longer shutter speeds and with longer lenses, I make a habit of doing it at all times.

"...allows you to obtain good steadiness even with a lightweight tripod..."

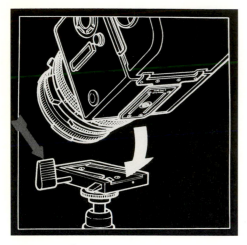

The use of a tripod coupling simplifies and speeds up photography. Such couplings can be used with most cameras. Some, however, are made for specific camera models.

"Another option you have on many cameras is to pre-set the shutter speed."

Selecting a Tripod

Maximum camera steadiness would call for the largest, heaviest studio tripod, but tripods used on location must also be carried. Therefore, you need a compromise between steadiness and portability. Such a tripod must be designed for fast, convenient operation so it is a pleasure, not a nuisance, to photograph.

An elevating extension is practical for lowering or raising the camera. The tripod, however, should bring the camera up to eye level without the need for using the extension. Do not consider the elevating extension as part of the tripod height because the three legs of the tripod should bring the camera up to eye level. Use the center post only for minor adjustments in the camera height. Any camera is much sturdier when it sits on three legs instead of a single post.

I prefer a ball head as it allows me to work faster than a head with separate adjustments and locking levers for side and front tilt. Use a tripod coupling that allows instant attaching and removing of the camera.

Tripod Substitutes

When you feel that some camera support is necessary, before rushing for the tripod, investigate other methods for steadying the camera such as leaning your body, arms or head against a wall, tree, or post, or resting camera or elbows on a surface. For low camera angles, lie on the ground and use your elbows as a support.

Excellent camera steadiness can also be obtained with a monopod which is easier to carry and quicker to set up than a tripod. The steadiest monopod operation is achieved when the foot is moved 2 or 3 feet forward with the monopod tilted towards the photographer.

In a way, the monopod then forms the third leg of a tripod with your own legs as the other two. You can obtain a steady grip with your eye pressed against the viewfinder, elbows pressed against your body, and either both hands on the camera or one hand on the camera and the other on top of the monopod.

Selection & Use of Shutter Speed

On automatic cameras, you can let the electronics in the camera decide on the shutter speed for you. This will, in many cases, produce an acceptable picture for you.

For serious work, however, you also want to maintain control over the shutter speed. You need not necessarily set the speed manually, but you want to know what the set shutter speed is before you press the release. In many cases, you may then want to change the aperture/shutter speed combination. Another option you have on many cameras is to pre-set the shutter speed.

Whatever the option, you should know at what shutter speed the image will be made. With a tripod-mounted camera, basically any shutter speed is usable. In hand-held work, you want a speed that is hopefully short enough to reduce or eliminate the danger of unsharpness due to camera motion.

The longest usable speed depends on your camera, your ability to hold a camera steady, whether the air is calm or the wind makes holding difficult, and the focal length of the lens. A good rule that works for many photographers is to keep the shutter speed at or shorter than the inverse of the focal length of the lens. For example, at 1/50, 1/60 or shorter for a 50 or 60mm lens, and at 1/250 when you use a 250mm lens. Due to the high resolution of today's films, I suggest shortening the speed even further, to 1/100 or 1/125 for a 50 or 60mm lens, especially on a medium format camera where you want to be assured of the utmost image sharpness.

I also suggest being more careful in using longer focal length lenses hand-held at any speed. Shutter speed must obviously be the first consideration in hand-held work. Matching the aperture for correct exposure is the

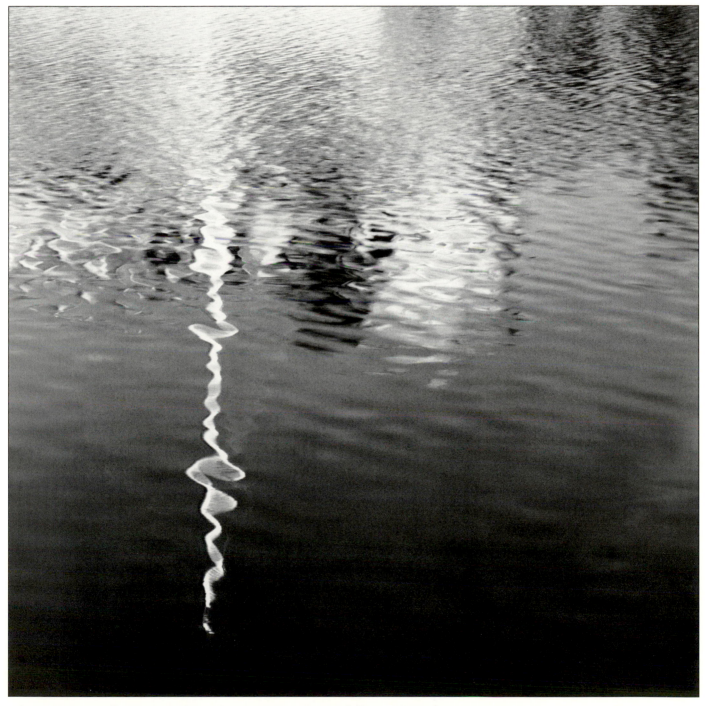

Blurred motion effects are not limited to streams and waterfalls. Anything that moves can make a fascinating image.

"...you create something that is different from the way we see the world."

second. When working with a tripod, selecting the aperture that produces the desired depth of field comes first, matching the shutter speed for exposure comes second.

Photographing Motion

When photographing moving subjects, the shutter is again the first consideration. You have a choice of selecting a speed that either freezes or blurs the motion. When you freeze the action, you create an image as we see the world with our eyes. With a longer speed that blurs the action, you not only convey in the image the feeling of motion, but you create something that is different from the way we see the world.

You create something that we cannot see with our eyes. I feel this is the reason why blurred motion images can be so beautiful and interesting. In a way, the shutter speed is perhaps the greatest feature that we have on every camera — it records a moving subject as only a camera can do. This applies not only to the typical moving subjects, such as water and sports action, but to anything that moves — leaves on a tree or grasses in a field moving in the wind, rides in an amusement park, reflections on water.

The amount of blur created by a certain shutter speed cannot be seen in the viewfinder of any camera. It can only be seen once it is recorded on the film. You must either photograph the subject at different shutter speeds and then evaluate the results on the film, or make test exposures on Polaroid film (if possible). Blurred motion is one application where the medium format camera with the possibility of attaching a Polaroid back at any time has a definite advantage.

To emphasize motion further, you may move the camera — an approach that also works beautifully in combination with a moving subject. It is a common approach in car, horse or track and field races where the camera follows the moving subject while making the exposure. The main blur is in the background, which emphasizes the motion and the speed.

To make this clearly visible, you need a background with details, with a contrast of light and dark colors. A plain background, such as the sky, does not work. This approach is not limited to sports. It works with any moving subject — a bird in flight, a child running through a field of tall grasses. The motion is frequently emphasized by the subject's motion moving in a different direction — the arms and legs in a runner or bicycle rider, the moving wings of a bird.

CHAPTER SIX

Lenses for Creating the Ultimate Sharpness

Since lenses create the image and are a main determining factor for image quality, it is to your advantage to know something about lens design and manufacturing, lens types, and image creating characteristics of lenses. This is especially true since there are many advertising claims that are confusing, and even misleading, to someone not familiar with optics.

The sharpness of any lens made anywhere in the world depends on two main factors: the lens design, and the accuracy and precision of the manufacturing. The latter is the main difference between ordinary and quality lenses.

Furthermore, the precision in assembling the elements into the lens barrel and the mechanical construction of the lens barrel are determining factors for the lens performance.

"...it is to your advantage to know something about lens design..."

Lens Design

All lenses are computer designed, which is nothing more than a computer tracing the light rays of the different colors through the different lens elements instead of doing it on paper. The computer does not design the lens, it only makes the calculations. What comes out depends on the information put into the computer by the lens designer.

Many different types of glass are available to the designer today, including the highly promoted low dispersion types The use of such glass does not automatically produce a better lens. It is the lens designer who must decide whether the use of such glass is beneficial.

Some lenses are promoted through the use of aspheric lens elements. Such elements, which are difficult to produce, again do not necessarily produce a better lens. A lens designer may find a solution to produce a lens of equal quality in other ways. Even the number of lens elements is not a determining factor. There are always more lens elements in a lens of larger aperture since it is more difficult to reduce all lens aberrations (faults) over the entire image area as the lens aperture increases. You are likely finding more elements in a wide angle lens, as the larger area coverage makes it more difficult to achieve corner to corner quality. But in any type of lens, a

"Only a lens test can reveal the lens performance."

good lens designer may come up with a better lens with fewer elements by applying the latest design techniques and using the latest types of glass. Only a lens test can reveal the lens performance.

Apochromatic Lenses

Camera lenses are corrected mainly for the blue and red colors of the spectrum. If well designed, such lenses produce superb image sharpness even on today's high resolution films. However, such lenses in the long focal length types may produce a color fringe, or a slight unsharpness in black and white on a sharp dividing line between bright and dark colors. This effect is seldom noticeable and practically never objectionable on a lens made by a well-known, reputable manufacturer.

Apochromatic types are corrected not only for blue and red, but green as well — which can be beneficial at least in long telephoto types. But as always, the quality of any lens depends on who designs it and who makes and assembles the lens elements.

Apochromatic lenses usually have some lens elements made from fluoride rather than glass. The focus setting depends on the temperature of the air, and the focusing ring may therefore turn beyond the infinity setting. Always focus such a lens visually on the focusing screen.

Wide Angle Design

Wide angle lenses on large format cameras and on non SLR 35mm and medium format types can be and usually are of the true optical design, the best for wide angle photography at far and close distances.

Since this design requires that the rear lens element is close to the film plane, such lenses cannot be used on SLR cameras. The mirror moving between the lens and film requires a long back focus. This can only be obtained on another wide angle design known as retrofocus.

All wide angle lenses on SLR cameras are of this design. While they probably have somewhat more distortion, they can have excellent quality, at least at long distances where wide angles are usually used. They are not the best types for close-up photography unless they have floating lens element. In such a design, some lens elements are or can be moved separately to improve image sharpness at closer distances. Since all floating lens element types are of a more recent design, they will likely also produce better quality at longer distances.

Zoom Lenses

Until recently, the general assumption was that a zoom lens does not produce the image sharpness of a fixed focal length type.

Even today, it can be said that there is no zoom lens that produces the sharpness of a fixed lens at every focal length over the entire zoom range. But many of today's zooms produce excellent quality, completely satisfactory for many applications. Only a film test can tell. When you make such a test, you must make it at different focal lengths.

The main distinguishing factor among zoom lenses is the zoom range — the ratio between the shortest and longest focal length. On medium format cameras, the range is limited for physical reasons. Zoom lenses for 35mm can go from a wide angle to a long telephoto, usually associated with a change of maximum aperture. While no general statement can be made, a

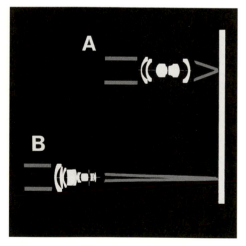

In an optically true wide angle design (top: A), the rear lens element is close to the film. Such lenses are therefore found only on rangefinder, large format and cameras with an optical viewfinder, not the SLR type.

Wide angle lenses on SLR cameras need the long distance between the film and rear element and must be of the so-called "retrofocus" design (bottom: B).

lens with a shorter zoom range may be preferable from a quality point of view. It is unquestionably more difficult to maintain good quality over a longer zoom range. Check published quality figures.

Quality at Different Distances

A lens designer must decide at what distance each lens should produce the very best image quality. The differences in quality at different distances depends on the lens design. It is hardly noticeable on an optically true wide angle design, but more obvious on the retrofocus type without floating lens elements.

Macro lenses that focus down to inches are available for many cameras. Their quality is undoubtedly good in close-up photography, but it should also be acceptable over the entire focusing range. If close-up photography is not your field, you may be better off with the non-macro type.

If close-up photography is your field, you may also note that some manufacturers have lenses that are specifically designed to provide the best image sharpness at close distances.

MTF Diagrams

The quality of lenses is usually expressed in resolution, or lines per millimeter that were recorded separately on the film. Photographic engineers and scientists, however, have found that the sharpness of an image as perceived by our eyes is more determined by the sharpness of the line edges rather than the resolution in number of lines. The modern way to publish the data for the lenses is in so-called MTF diagrams. They combine resolution

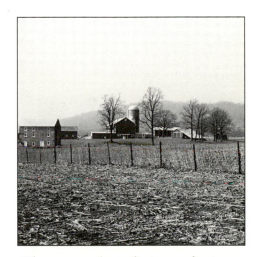

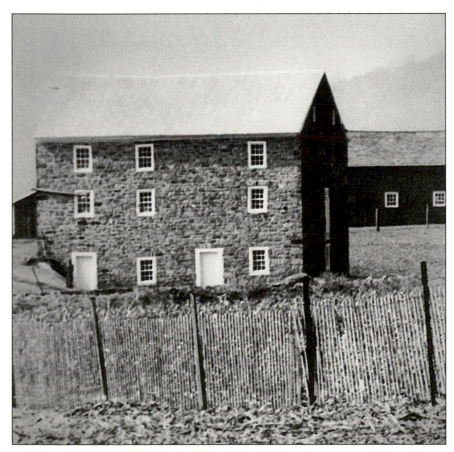

When you evaluate the image sharpness, always check the center and corners. The photo to the left is what you see when evaluating the original image (above) with a 10x magnifying glass. While there is a slight fall off in sharpness at the far edge, this quality is excellent for a wide angle lens with the aperture wide open. Especially considering that the enlarged portion is at the very edge of the original image. Taken with a 6x6cm medium format camera.

with edge sharpness. Some lens manufacturers publish such data. There are, however, no standards among manufacturers. Some manufacturers show the curves that the computer produced, others the results that are actually produced by the finished lens. This non-standardized practice makes it difficult or impossible to compare lenses made by different manufacturers.

The curves, however, indicate the sharpness differences between the center of the image and the edges of a specific lens, or the sharpness improvement when the aperture is closed if the diagrams are published for different apertures. The curves can also show, for example, the sharpness differences between close and far distances if published for both distances.

Multi-Coating

All modern lenses are multi-coated to reduce lens flare and to increase the contrast and color saturation in the images. To what extent the coating reduces flare, however, depends completely on the lens design and varies from one lens to another.

Multi-coating does not eliminate or reduce the need for using lens shades for one reason: multi-coating and shades serve different purposes. The multi-coating is there to help reduce reflections from the light that goes through the lens to create the image. The shade is there to eliminate the light that is not needed for creating the image. Regardless of your equipment, use the best possible shade on every one of your lenses.

For some cameras, you can select bellows shades where the bellows can be extended more or less to match the focal length of the lens. Made from a folded bellows, they usually provide the best shading.

Using a most effective shade is essential not only when photographing towards the sun or other light source, but also on overcast days when white skies are very bright, when photographing in the snow, sand, or near water, and especially when photographing against white backgrounds in the studio.

Light can also be reflected onto the film from the camera interior, a reason some manufacturers coat the interior with a dull, dark finish.

Illumination

A photographer's main concern is image sharpness. A second concern must be image brightness. On standard and longer focal length lenses, image brightness is usually even from corner to corner.

Wide angle lenses frequently show a darkening in the corners which can be objectionable in many pictures, especially those that have large areas of equal brightness, such as a sky. Some lens manufacturers publish the illumination data. If not, test wide angle lenses for image brightness.

Image Distortion

Distortion is the lens's ability or inability to record straight lines as straight lines over the entire film area. Straight lines near the edges that appear curved inward are referred to as "pin-cushion distortion;" if curved outward we call it "barrel distortion." Distortion needs to be considered mainly when photographing buildings and products.

Wide Angle Distortion

Images taken with wide angle lenses on any camera often show a distortion in subjects on the edges or corners of the picture. People's faces look

> "All modern lenses are multi-coated to reduce lens flare..."

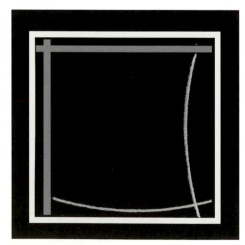

If a lens is not properly corrected for distortion, straight lines close to the edges will be recorded curved. This is the only kind of distortion that is the fault of the lens design.

distorted, a round chandelier in the corner is egg shaped. This so-called wide angle distortion happens when photographing a three dimensional subject with any camera and wide angle lens. The distortion, however, is not caused by the lens. It must be blamed on the film plane being flat in the camera, thus "stretching out" such three dimensional subjects at the sides or corners. It cannot be avoided regardless of the camera or wide angle lens you are using. Try to improve the picture by changing the composition so that such subjects do not appear at the edges or corners.

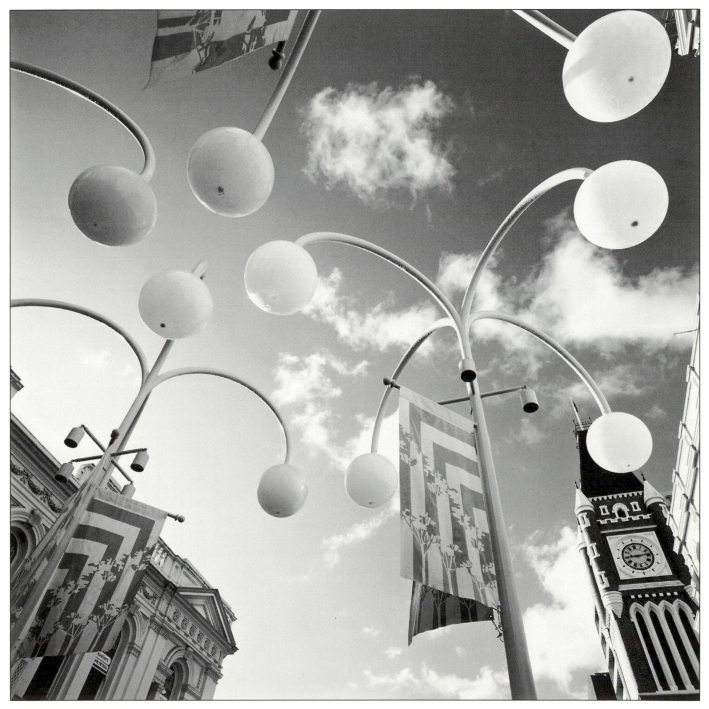

With wide angle lenses, objects close to the edges or corners appear distorted. It is not a fault of the lens and happens on any camera with any wide angle lens.

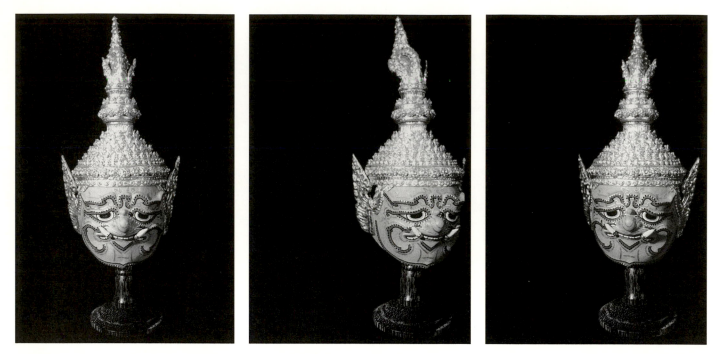

The photo on the left shows the subject as it appears in the center on the film. The photo in the middle shows the subject on the side, taken with a 50mm lens (equivalent to 32mm on 35mm) on a medium format camera. Notice the distortion. The photo on the right is the same subject at the side taken with the same lens, but the head is turned towards the camera lens. Distortion is barely visible.

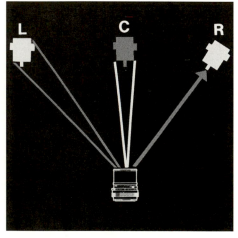

Wide angle distortion is further emphasized because the lens sees the subject at the edges differently from those in the center. The lens looks at the side of a person's head on the left (L), not the front of the face as in the center (C). The distortion can be reduced by turning the subject so the lens looks also at the front of their face (R).

Besides the flat film plane, there is a second reason that enhances this distortion of three dimensional subjects. The wide angle lens sees the subject in the center from a different angle than the subjects at the edges. In a group picture, the lens looks at the front of the faces of the people in the center, but at the side of their heads on those standing on the left or right.

You can reduce the distortion by turning the people so they all look straight towards the lens, so the lens "sees" the front of the face on everyone in the group. The same approach can be used in a line-up of products. Since wide angle distortion is not the fault of the lens, it does not occur when photographing flat, two dimensional subjects — in copying, for example.

Teleconverters

Teleconverters come mainly in two types: 2x and 1.4x. They are mounted between the camera and lens. A 2x extender doubles the focal length of any lens resulting in a 500mm focal length when combined with a lens of 250mm focal length. A 1.4 extender lengthens the focal length by 1.4x.

Teleconverters are usually designed to work with all focal length lenses in a camera system, but there naturally must be a compromise since the different focal length lenses have different lens designs. The image sharpness will undoubtedly vary somewhat, depending on the lens with which it is combined.

Today, however, we have teleconverters that produce excellent quality, so they no longer need to be considered the "poor man's choice for a tele lens." Such converters may have as many or even more lens elements than some prime lenses and can be made to the same quality standards. Consequently, they cost as much, or almost as much, as a prime lens. Even if a teleconverter costs as much, you still have the benefit of being able to combine it with different focal length lenses and obtaining long focal lengths without having to carry the heavier tele lenses.

Any teleconverter can only produce good image quality when combined with a high quality lens because the teleconverter emphasizes the faults of the basic lens.

Tele-extenders also create a loss of light equivalent to two f-stops with any 2x extender. Combined with a lens with an $f/2.8$ aperture, the combination will have a maximum aperture of $f/5.6$. From a photographic point of

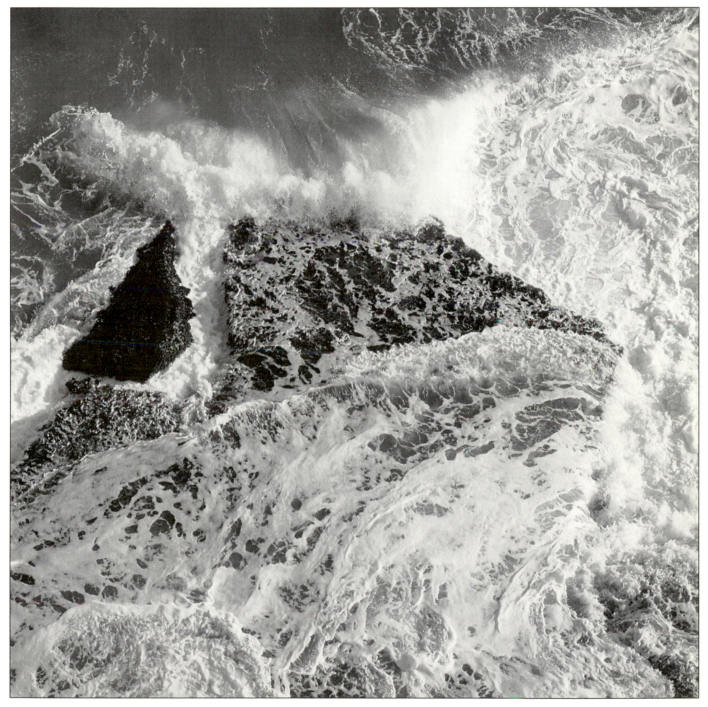

Image quality with a 1.4x tele-extender.

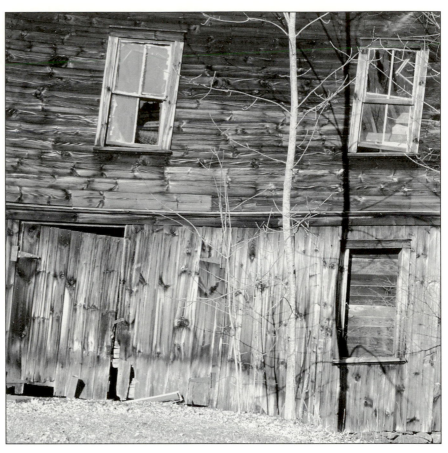

Image quality with a 2x tele-extender.

view, the loss of light is frequently only one f-stop, as longer focal length lenses also tend to be slower. As an example, a 120mm lens may be $f/4$ resulting in a 240mm $f/8$ lens when combined with the 2x extender. A 250mm lens, on the other hand, may have a maximum aperture of $f/5.6$. A 1.4x extender loses one f-stop.

Teleconverters also have a very valuable advantage: the focusing range of the lens is maintained. If, for example, a 180mm lens focuses down to 5 feet, it still focuses down to 5 feet when combined with the converter. With a 2x converter, we have a 360mm focal length lens focusing down to 5 feet, which may very well be much closer than the minimum focusing distance on a longer telephoto.

The depth of field scale on the 180mm lens no longer applies since the depth of field is now equivalent to that of a 360mm lens. On the other hand, the shooting aperture is two f-stops less than set on the lens; $f/11$ with the lens set at $f/5.6$. The depth of field at 360mm and $f/11$ happens to be very similar to the depth of field at 180mm and $f/5.6$.

For all practical purposes then, you can use the depth of field scale on the lens (180mm in this example) for the aperture that is set on the lens ($f/5.6$ in this case).

"...the focusing range of the lens is maintained."

CHAPTER SEVEN

Effective Use of Lenses & Lens Controls

Aperture and focusing are the two main operating controls on a lens. Shutter speed is the third if the lens has a shutter — otherwise it is part of the camera.

Choice of Lens Aperture

Image sharpness improves somewhat, especially on the edges, as the aperture is closed down. Even with the aperture wide open, the loss of sharpness should never be objectionable or even noticeable under normal viewing conditions of the final print or transparency. If it is, buy a better lens.

It should never be necessary to close the lens aperture more than 2 f-stops to have perfect sharpness even on the edges and when viewing the original under a 10x magnifying glass. Top quality lenses can give you such results with the lens aperture wide open in applications for which the lenses are designed.

In any case, it should never be necessary to close down the aperture simply for the purpose of obtaining satisfactory corner to corner quality.

Image Sharpness at Small Apertures

When light goes through a very small opening, some light rays are refracted. This happens even in a pinhole camera. That phenomenon explains the frequently heard statement that the lens aperture should never be closed completely.

While this is theoretically correct, it need not be considered with high quality lenses made by a reputable manufacturer. Such manufacturers limit the minimum aperture to a point where the light refraction does not create a visible loss of sharpness. That explains why such lenses may only close down to $f/16$ or $f/22$. If you need to close the lens aperture completely on such a lens to obtain the desired depth of field, close it.

You may decide on the lens aperture mainly based on the desired shutter speed (in hand-held work for example) but for the majority of pictures, the choice should be based on the desired depth of field. This can be obtained from the engraved scales on the lens or from charts.

"...loss of sharpness should never be objectionable or even noticeable..."

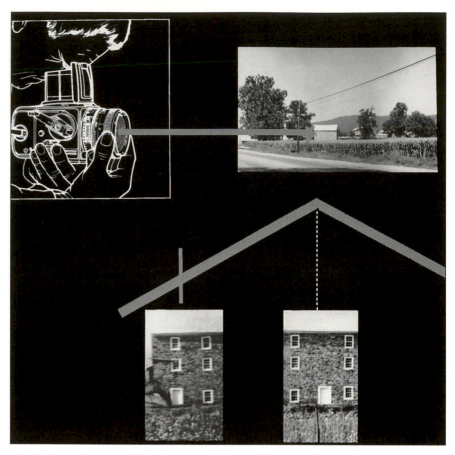

Only the subject at which the lens is focused has maximum sharpness in the image. There is a visible loss of sharpness in subjects closer or farther from the camera, even if they are within the depth of field range.

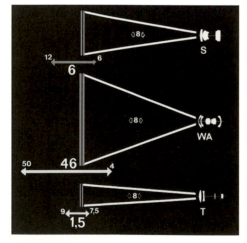

When different focal length lenses are used from the same distance, the wide angle (WA) has more depth of field than the standard (S) or telephoto (T). Each lens, however, also covers a different area, creating a completely different image.

Depth of Field

When a lens is set to a certain distance, only the subject point at that distance is recorded critically sharp on the film. Anything closer or farther is progressively less sharp. There is, however, a range in front and beyond the set distance where subjects are recorded with acceptable sharpness. This means that they will still appear sharp to our eyes if the negative or transparency is enlarged to an "ordinary" size.

On today's high resolution films, you will see the loss of sharpness within the depth of field range when you examine the original under a 10x magnifying glass, especially on the larger medium format originals. Subjects close to the limit of the depth of field range appear outright unsharp under the magnifier. Depth of field charts were calculated years ago when films were not that great and as far as I know, they have never been updated.

If you do critical work on today's high resolution films, I suggest that you do not use the entire depth of field range or stop the lens aperture down at least one more *f*-stop than is necessary to cover the desired range. If a specific part within your scene (the mountains in the distance, for example) is to be recorded with the utmost sharpness, set the focusing ring at that distance; don't rely on depth of field.

Depth of field is a calculated figure and is not related to the lens design or lens performance. However, a lens that is critically sharp may perhaps appear to have less depth of field. That is only because the fall off in the sharpness is more obvious on such a lens.

A frequent statement is that telephoto lenses have less depth of field than those of shorter focal length. This is correct when the different lenses are used to photograph a subject or scene from the same distance. If used this way, however, the wide angle lens covers a much larger area than the standard or telephoto. The lenses create completely different images.

If the different focal length lenses are used to cover the same area, that is with the wide angle closer to the subject and the telephoto farther away, all lenses produce the same depth of field at the same aperture. Keep this in mind, especially when you photograph a subject of a specific size (a portrait, for example) or in close-up or product photography.

Regardless of the lens or close-up accessory, the range of sharpness is the same. When using a longer lens however, the fall off in sharpness beyond the depth of field is more obvious than with a shorter focal length, so you have a chance to blur the background more or less.

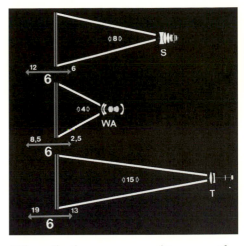

When the lenses are used to cover the same area, all lenses have the same depth of field at the same aperture.

Composing Group Pictures

Some photographers seem to be under the impression that the people in a group picture should be arranged on a curved rather than a straight line, especially when wide angle lenses are used. The reasoning is that the people

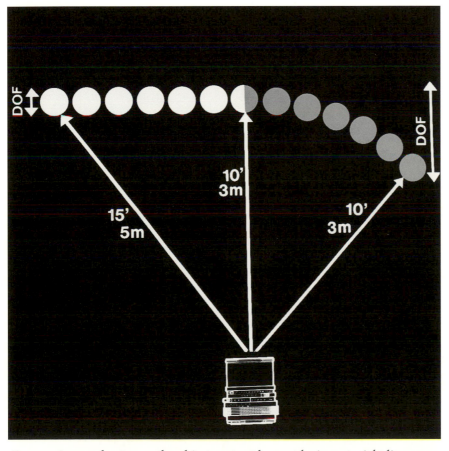

For maximum sharpness, the objects or people must be in a straight line, even though the people at the edge are farther (15 feet) from the lens. The people can be lined up in a curved plane, but the aperture of the lens needs to be then reduced to produce more depth of field (DOF).

on the outside are farther from the lens than those in the center, perhaps 15 feet instead of the 10 feet in the center. Arranged on a curved line, everyone can be the same distance from the lens and will therefore be sharp. But this is not correct as far as sharpness is concerned. Every lens is designed to produce a sharp image on the flat film plane, from any flat subject in front of the lens, whether it is the flat wall of a building, the text arranged on a flat copy board, or a group of people.

For best edge to edge sharpness, align the people on a flat plane. You can perhaps align the people in a circle for better flash illumination. However, if so, you must close the lens aperture to provide the necessary depth of field — from 7 to 10 feet in the aforementioned example.

Hyperfocal Distance

Hyperfocal distance is related to depth of field and is usually described as the focus setting that produces the maximum depth of field. Hyperfocal distance is the distance setting that produces depth of field up to infinity at the set lens aperture. Since most lenses have engraved depth of field scales, it is not necessary to have hyperfocal distance charts.

Any lens is set to the hyperfocal distance when the infinity mark on the focusing ring is set opposite the aperture marking on the depth of field scale that corresponds to the aperture that is set on the lens. The hyperfocal distance is the reading that is opposite the index.

The minimum depth of field distance is opposite the corresponding aperture marking to the left of the index. While this setting produces the maximum depth of field and depth of field to infinity, keep in mind that subjects at infinity will be acceptably, but not critically sharp.

Plane of Focus

The range of sharpness in a photographic image can also be changed by tilting the lens or film plane in relation to the other. This is a well-known practice in large format photography where it is usually done by tilting the lens plane. Some shift lenses also allow tilting, thus offering this capability in 35mm. In the medium format, the possibility exists either with a flexible bellows between camera body and lens or with a special camera body having a flexible bellows between lens and film frame (like a view camera).

This tilt control allows more sharpness from front to back (or left to right) without changing the lens aperture. The principle is well-known to large format photographers: you have the maximum range of sharpness when the lines extended from the film plane and the lens plane meet at a common point on a line extended from the subject plane.

This control, however, is possible only in one plane, and in a flat plane only. If an object protrudes above this plane (a tree trunk, a house, a tall vase in a still life), the protruding object must be kept in sharp focus with the lens's depth of field, closing down the aperture to keep that object within the range of sharpness.

Without such a special camera or lens, you can take advantage of this concept in a limited fashion. On a normal camera, the plane of focus is parallel to the film plane. Rather than photographing a flat landscape straight on when the plane of focus (the film plane) is 90 degrees to the subject plane, try to do it from a higher angle, and angle the camera downward. This brings the film plane more parallel to the plane of the landscape.

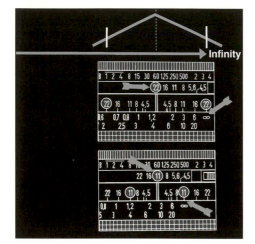

A lens is set to the hyperfocal distance when the infinity mark on the focusing ring is set opposite the aperture marking on the depth of field scale that corresponds to the aperture set on the lens. The hyperfocal distance is the distance opposite the index mark.

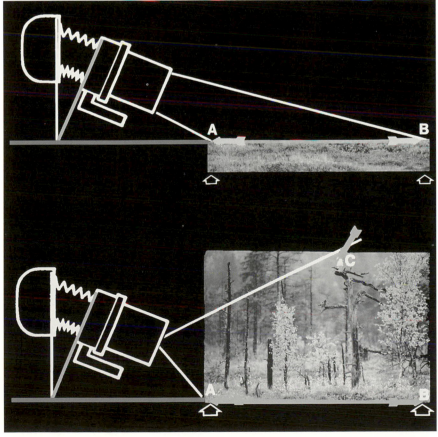

The range of sharpness is usually determined by the depth of field which depends on the aperture setting on the lens. By shifting the film plane in relation to the lens plane, the range of sharpness can be greatly extended at the same lens aperture.

When tilting the film or lens plane, the sharpness range can be increased only along one straight plane. A subject at C will not be sharp unless it is within the depth of field range of the lens. You could, of course, also shift the film or lens plane along the axis A-C, but then subjects at B would be out of focus.

Manual Stop Down Control

For serious photography, the lenses on your SLR camera must have a manual stop down control. This control will allow you to see on the focusing screen how the image will be recorded on the film at the set aperture, or to decide on a specific aperture by evaluating the image on the screen. Some instructional material will tell you that the control allows you to see the amount of depth of field. I disagree. As already explained, the acceptable sharpness within the depth of field range is based on a certain degree of enlargement.

On the camera, you are looking at a small focusing screen: 24x36mm in 35mm, 55x55mm on a square medium format camera. You are also viewing the image on a focusing screen which does not allow seeing the finest details. When the aperture is closed down, you reduce the image brightness, which makes the situation still worse.

To determine depth of field, I suggest that you consult the depth of field scales. The manual stop down control will give you a very good idea of what is sharp and what is not, and how much sharpness or unsharpness is created in the fore or background, revealing disturbing fore or background elements which may not be noticed at the maximum aperture.

Since backgrounds are an important part of many of our images, this fact alone justifies using the stop down control for evaluating our images on the focusing screen. In short, the manual stop down control gives you a very clear idea of what the final image will look like without having to record it on film.

A medium or large format camera has a distinguished advantage over 35mm as far as image evaluation is concerned. The larger focusing screen

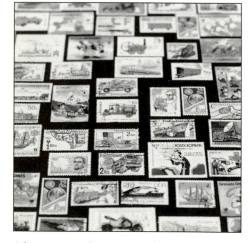

The image above was photographed at f/8 with a short telephoto lens. The image to the right was photographed with the same lens at the same aperture but with the film plane shifted to maintain the sharpness from top to bottom.

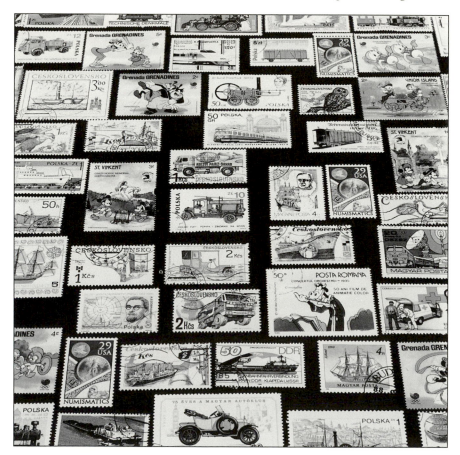

provides a better and more effective image evaluation with the aperture wide open or closed down — and on some cameras you can also evaluate the image with both eyes open, using the standard focusing hood.

Background & Foreground Sharpness

While the actual depth of field is the same with any lens when covering the same area, longer lenses magnify the background area and thus also magnify the degree of background unsharpness. With a shorter focal length lens, the background may be only slightly blurred. The same applies to foregrounds which are beyond the depth of field.

You can frequently produce effective images outdoors by planning the composition around some completely blurred foreground objects — flowers, leaves, grasses. This approach works especially well in color where the foreground can add an effective touch of color surrounding the main subject, in a portrait, for example.

Out of focus foregrounds are usually best when blurred completely so they are not even recognizable. If the foreground is blurred just a little, it might look like a mistake. If the standard lens does not provide enough blur, go to a telephoto.

Zoom Lenses & Zoom Effects

Everything described about the use of different focal length lenses also applies to zooms. Zoom lenses simply give you the possibility of obtaining the different focal lengths by using the zoom control.

On a true zoom lens, the image stays in focus while zooming. I recommend, however, that you do the visual focusing on the screen always with the lens set to the longest focal length. The image is more magnified, so focusing is more accurate and faster. You can also see more accurately at which part of the scene or subject you focus. Once focused, you can take the picture at whatever focal length gives you the desired composition.

Zoom lenses also give you the opportunity to create zoom effects by changing the focal length — moving the zoom control while the shutter is open. Changing the focal length changes the image size, thus creating the typical zoom image with streaks — something that can only be created with the camera, not with our eyes. You need a fairly long shutter speed that gives you enough time to move the zoom control while the shutter is open. I usually use ½ or 1 second.

When zooming from the shorter to the longer focal lengths, the resulting streaks go from the center to the outside of the image. You can make them go from the outside to the center by zooming the opposite direction. The effect also depends on whether you zoom fast or slow and whether you zoom during the entire exposure time or only part of it.

Zooming over the entire exposure time, 1 second perhaps, creates mainly a blur. Most images are more effective by leaving the lens at one focal length for about half the exposure (½ sec.) with a 1 second exposure time, and zooming only over the remaining time (the remaining ½ sec.). This approach produces a sharp image of the subject with the streaks added and surrounding it. Zoom effects are most successful with contrasty subjects — lighted signs, highlights on water surfaces, street or car lights. The streaks produced by the highlights are best visible when they cross a darker area.

"Out of focus foregrounds are usually best when blurred completely..."

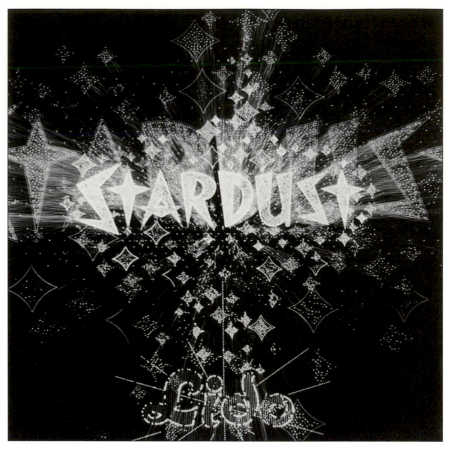

Changing the focal length on a zoom lens while the shutter is open produces unique and dramatic images. The photo was taken with a one second exposure.

Lenses for Area Coverage

Area coverage is the main difference between lenses of different focal lengths. Wide angle lenses cover a larger area than standard types, tele lenses cover less from the same camera position. Area coverage is frequently the only reason to select a specific focal length. A lens that has twice the focal length covers an area half as wide and high on the same film format.

Two points to remember: the focal length of a lens is a fixed value, and it can only be changed by adding or taking away lens elements. That means the focal length is the same regardless for what film format it is being used. An 80mm lens from a medium format camera is still an 80mm lens when used on a 35mm camera or on an enlarger.

Lenses are also designed to cover a certain film area. This is known as covering power. 35mm lenses are basically designed to cover the 24x36mm frame area and do not usually produce satisfactory image quality and illumination if put on a medium format camera. A lens designed for a larger format should, however, work beautifully for a smaller format using only the center area of the image. That is why adapters are available for using some medium format lenses on some 35mm cameras.

Image Perspective

Perspective is the size relationship between subjects close to and far from the camera. With our eyes, we see the world in one specific perspective, call

"Lenses are also designed to cover a certain film area."

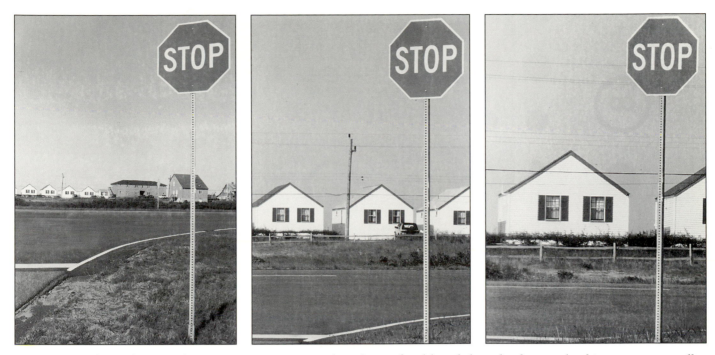

Camera to subject distance determines perspective. With a shorter focal length lens, background subjects appear smaller and thus farther away. The background can be made to appear larger and closer by using a longer focal length lens from a longer distance to maintain the size of the foreground subject, the stop sign. The photo to the left was taken with a short telephoto lens, the middle photo was taken with a long telephoto lens and the photo to the right was taken with a wide angle lens.

it "normal." Pictures taken with a normal (standard) lens on a camera (50mm for 35, 80mm for a 6x6 medium format camera) show the world pretty much as we see it with our eyes. That is why it is called "standard."

By switching to a wide angle lens and at the same time moving closer to the foreground subject, we can record the foreground in the same size. The background subjects are now recorded smaller and they appear farther away. We have changed the size relationship, changed the perspective. We no longer recorded a "normal" image as we see it with our eyes.

We can also maintain the foreground subject size by photographing with a longer focal length lens from a longer distance. The background subjects now appear larger and closer to the camera. The mountains in the background can be made three or four times larger, making them more dominant and more dramatic.

Use the standard lens to create an image as we see the world. Use the shorter and longer lenses to create something different as only the camera can do.

The explanations of the use of lenses probably gives the impression that perspective is determined by the focal length of the lens. Not so. It is determined by the distance to the foreground subject. But you need the wide angle lens to cover the foreground subject from a short distance, a telephoto to do the same from a longer distance.

Background Coverage

With a shorter focal length lens, background subjects are not only recorded smaller but you also cover a larger background area. With a longer focal length lens, you cover a smaller background area. Keep this in mind

"The larger background area reveals the location..."

because backgrounds are an important part in many of our images. How much we cover may very well determine the effectiveness of our images.

Wide angle lenses have become popular in outdoor portrait photography. The larger background area reveals the location, making it an important part of the image. I call this a "true location portrait."

Longer focal length lenses allow the elimination of distracting background elements like cars, billboards, people, *et cetera*. With a longer lens, just a slight change in the camera angle can bring a completely different background area behind the main subject.

Effective Wide Angle Photography

Wide angle lenses can be used to cover more of the subject or scene. When doing this, however, also try to accomplish something else — enhancing the three dimensional aspect of the scene. You can do this by including effective foreground elements in the composition.

The foreground subject can be anything — a rock or rock formation, flowers, weeds, a tree stump, a fence, *et cetera*. Such a composition emphasizes the use of wide angle lenses, adds depth and a three dimensional feeling to the image, producing a true wide angle image — the best and main reason for considering the use of a wide angle lens.

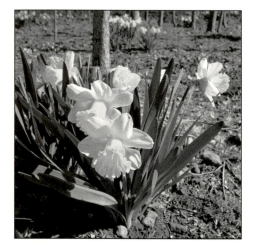

Wide angle lenses can be effective for close-ups (above) because of the large background coverage, making the surrounding area a part of the image. Wide angle lenses should be used not just to cover larger areas, but to enhance the perspective, the depth, and the three dimensional aspect of the image (right). Including dominant foreground subjects can accomplish this.

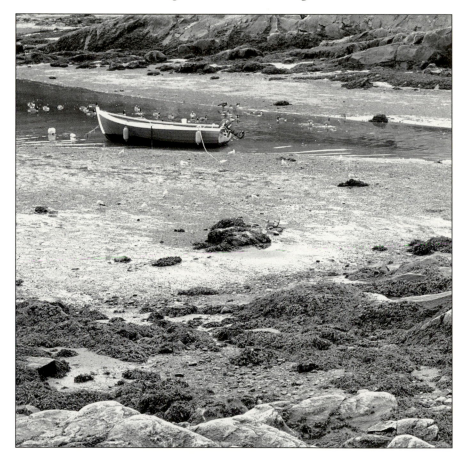

Fisheye Photography

Fisheye lenses provide an additional opportunity for creating images which are different from the way we see the world. The diagonal angle of view of such lenses is much greater (usually 180 degrees) and completely unrelated to the vertical and horizontal coverage regardless of their focal length. They cover diagonally a much larger area than wide angle lenses of the same focal length. Consequently, they produce images with curved horizontal and vertical lines off the center area. This is what gives fisheye images their particular touch.

There are two completely different types of fisheye lens designs. One type produces a circular image, covering only the center portion of the film frame. The attention is created by the circular shape of the image which becomes

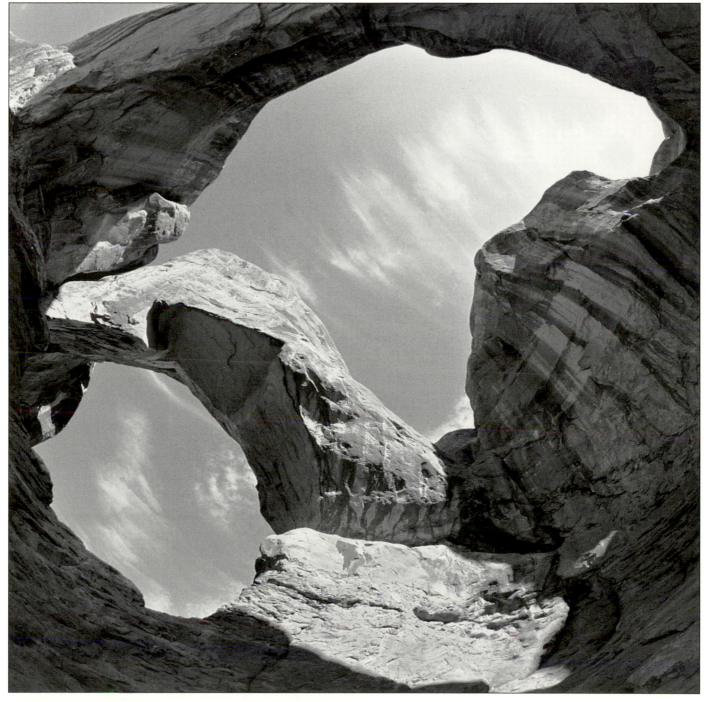

A full frame fisheye lens can produce images that do not have the typical fisheye look but can be effective because of the 180 degrees diagonal coverage.

"They can be great tools for creating unusual images..."

monotonous quickly. Such lenses are of limited value in serious photography. The other type is a full frame fisheye, which covers the entire film area. They can be great tools for creating unusual images of ordinary subjects.

Fisheye and Non Fisheye Images

A good full frame fisheye lens can cover the entire film area with excellent sharpness and illumination. The typical curved lines surrounding the center area provide the best reason for using such a lens. At the same time, keep in mind that the curved lines are only created off center. Straight lines going exactly through the center (vertically, horizontally or diagonally) remain perfectly straight. So you can also create images that hardly reveal the use of the fisheye lens.

You can place the horizon in a landscape, or a tree trunk in the center and the image may almost look like an "ordinary" picture — but only "almost." While the image may not have the typical fisheye look, the 180 degree diagonal angle of view of the lens covers a much larger area than any wide angle lens. If you compose a round subject (the face of a clock, for example), perfectly centered, you also maintain the perfectly round shape of the clock. The possibility of producing such "non fisheye" images is the second advantage of the full frame fisheye design.

Perspective Control

When photographing subjects with parallel vertical lines, such as the lines of a building, the vertical lines are recorded parallel only if the film plane is parallel to the subject, the building. Tilting a camera results in

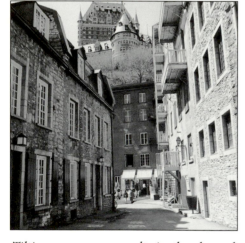

Tilting a camera results in the slanted verticals that are unacceptable in most architectural pictures (above). Perspective control allows covering the same area without tilting the camera (right).

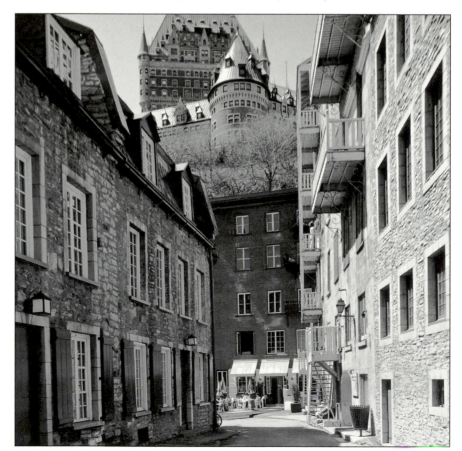

slanted lines. While this may be a perfectly normal view as it also happens when we tilt our head to look at a skyscraper, it can look like a technical fault if the lines are only slightly slanted, making it obvious that the camera was tilted just to get the entire building into the picture. Slanted verticals can be effective — but only to create something different.

It is often possible to "straighten out" verticals by photographing from a longer distance with a longer focal length lens. The longer distance eliminates or reduces the need for tilting the camera. If this is not possible, a lens or tele-converter with perspective control (PC) can help.

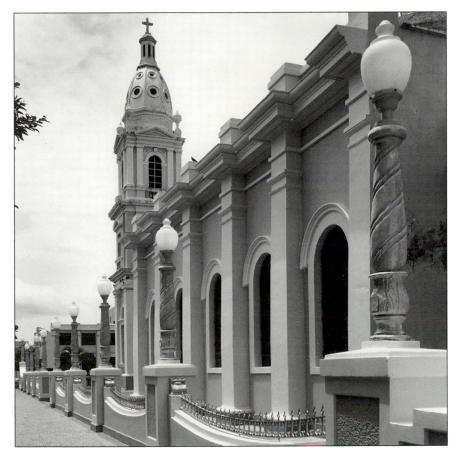

Perspective control in a 35mm or medium format camera can produce very professional architectural images without the need for carrying a large format camera. This photo was taken in Puerto Rico.

Perspective Control Lenses

On PC lenses or PC teleconverters, a mechanical arrangement allows shifting the optics upwards and downwards to cover more on top or bottom of the subject without tilting the camera. To be able to do this, the PC lens or lens combined with a PC converter must have a larger covering power than the image area on the film. The lens can then be moved out of the optical center without objectionable sharpness loss or vignetting.

Vertical lines can also be straightened out by tilting the lens or film plane. You can tilt the camera to cover the building to the top, then straighten out the verticals by tilting the film plane so it is parallel to the building. Some PC lenses provide this control and so do special camera bodies in the medium format field, as well as practically all large format cameras.

"Vertical lines can also be straightened out by tilting the lens or film plane."

CHAPTER EIGHT
Achieving the Ultimate Exposure

The ultimate quality in a photographic image can only be obtained if the negative or transparency is properly exposed. A seasoned photographer may determine the lens settings for correct exposure based on experience. Most photographers, on the other hand, will rely on the reading from an exposure meter (which can be a separate meter or one built into the camera), or on the automatic exposure control built into many 35mm or medium format cameras.

Metering Methods

Exposure information can be obtained either by measuring the amount of light that falls on the subject (incident meters) or the light that is reflected from the subject (reflected types).

Incident meters have a dome-like fixture measuring the light that falls on the subject from all the different directions. They have the advantage that the reading is unaffected by the brightness or the color of the subject. The reading is therefore the same — regardless of the color or brightness of the subject — and the reading is usually correct, regardless whether the subject is white, black, gray or any other color. There is not much more you must learn about the use of an incident meter.

Incident meter readings are made by pointing the metering cell from the subject towards the camera lens. The meter reading therefore has to be taken from the position of the subject, not from the camera.

While this is usually no drawback in the studio, or in some location work from a tripod, it is a time-consuming process and practically useless for hand-held work in different lighting situations.

Reflected meters have the advantage that the meter reading can be taken from the camera position, which is helpful outdoors — especially in hand-held work. A reflected meter reading is, however, affected not only by the amount of light that falls on the subject, but also by the color and brightness of the subject, giving a higher reading for light subjects and a lower one for darker ones. To obtain perfect exposures with reflected light meters, you must know a little more about the proper use of the meter. A reflected meter can be a hand-held type, or can be built into a camera.

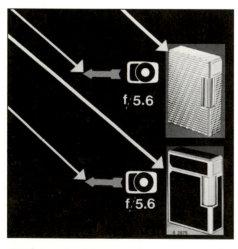

With an incident exposure meter, the meter reading is determined only by the amount of light that falls on the subject and is the same for bright and dark subjects.

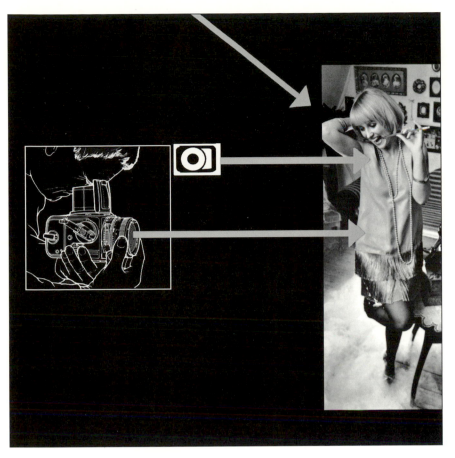

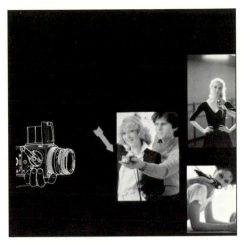

Most incident meter readings must be made from the position of the subject (above). Reflected meter readings can be made from the camera position which allows faster shooting and is more practical for hand-held work (left). The original photo in the illustration to the left is by Carrebye-Fotografi A/S from a Hasselblad Wide Angle brochure.

Using Exposure Meters

Any exposure meter can give the photographer the correct lens settings, but only if used properly. With any meter, we the photographers must determine what area to measure, then interpret the reading and decide whether it is correct or an adjustment must be made. This applies even to the use of built-in meters.

Light Reflectance and Average Subject Brightness

With reflected and built-in meters, the color and brightness of the subject must always be considered when taking a meter reading. The measuring cell in such a metering device is adjusted at the factory for a middle gray or any color and shade that reflects about 18% of the light. That is what the Kodak Gray Card does. The meter reading is, therefore, only correct when an 18% reflectance area is measured. When measuring a darker or brighter area, an adjustment must be made with any film, transparency or negative type. When measuring brighter areas, increase exposure (open the aperture or lengthen the shutter speed). For a meter reading of white snow, for example, increase exposure by 2EV values or 2 *f*-stops. When measuring darker areas, decrease exposure (close aperture or shorten shutter speed). For dark green, dark red or brown, decrease exposure by 1EV value or 1 *f*-stop. The above applies regardless of the film in the camera (negative or transparency).

What is Average Brightness?

The Kodak gray card is the most accurate reference for an 18% reflectance. Most subjects that we photograph are not in gray tones, but in

"When measuring brighter areas, increase exposure."

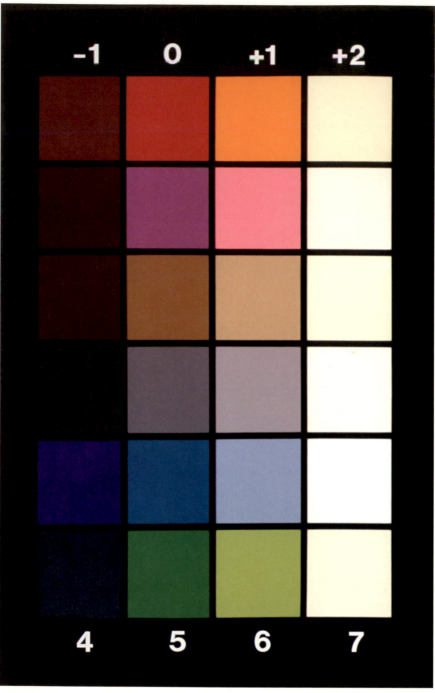

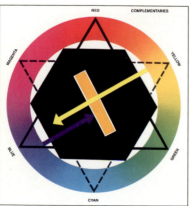

Above: The reflectance values for different shades and colors. The colors in the column (0) reflect 18% and therefore give the correct exposure with a reflected or built-in light meter. Meter readings of the colors in columns +1 or +2 need a one or two stop increase respectively in exposure. Reflected meter readings of the darker colors in column -1 need a one stop decrease in exposure, close the aperture one stop. The numbers on the bottom refer to equivalent zone values, zone 5 for 18% reflectance.

Left: In b&w photography, a color filter lightens the subjects that have the same color as the filter, and darkens those that have a color on the opposite side of the color wheel. A yellow filter lightens yellow and darkens blue, for example.

Opposite page: Full frame fisheye images that cover the entire 35mm or medium format film area are much more effective than the circular images produced by an ordinary fisheye lens.

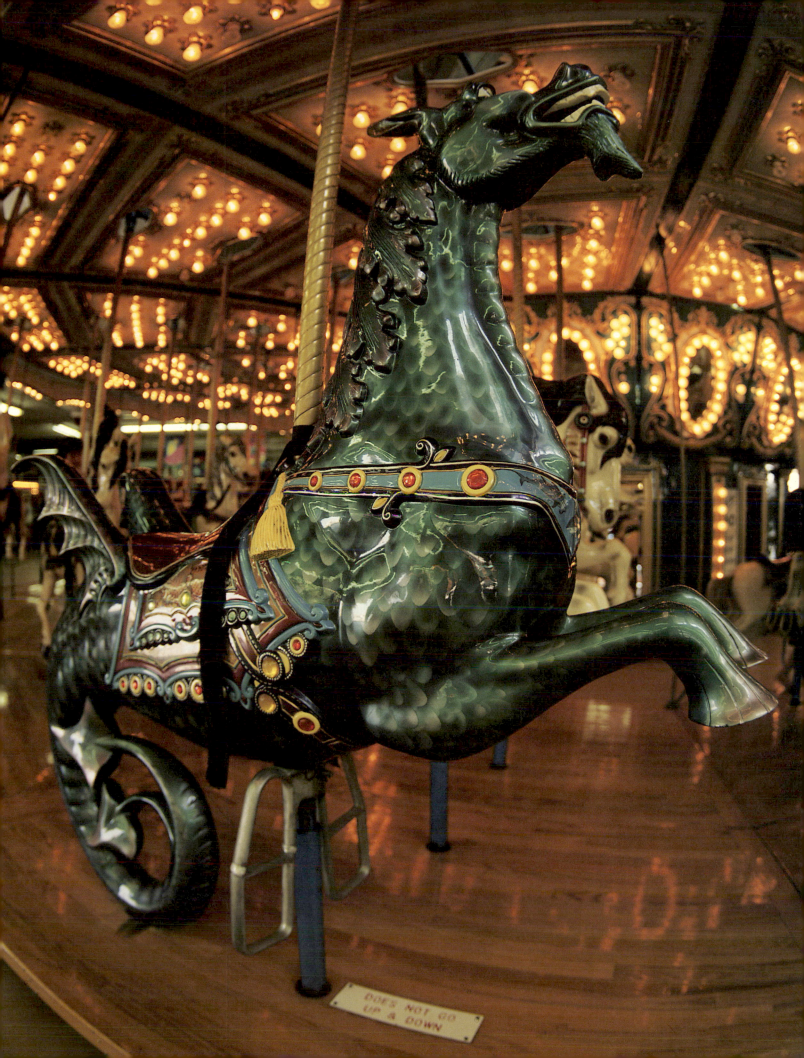

DOES NOT GO
UP & DOWN

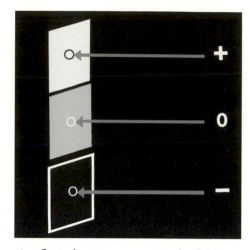

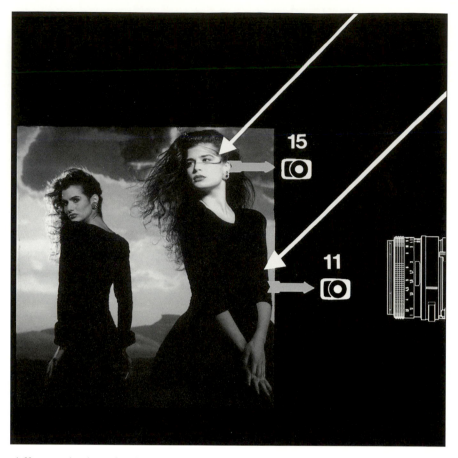

A reflected meter, or a meter built into a camera, will give a higher reading when pointed at a brighter subject area, even if the same amount of light falls on the light and dark areas (right). A meter reading with a reflected or built-in meter is correct only when the reading comes from an area that reflects 18% of the light. When the meter reading is made of brighter areas, exposure must be increased; when made of darker areas, exposure must be decreased, the aperture must be closed down (above). The photo used in the illustration on the right was taken by Steven Talley from Forum 4/90.

different shades of colors. Each color reflects a different amount of light. The printed color chart illustrates which colors and shades are average brightness (Column 0) and which are brighter or darker, with the necessary increase or decrease in EV or f-stops values (from +2 to -1) indicated on top. Use this chart as a guide. You will quickly learn to evaluate subject brightness.

The Metering Approach

Exposing for Negative Film

Negatives (black and white or color) must have adequate details in the primary shadow areas, otherwise they will not produce satisfactory black and white or color prints. Negative films (black and white or color), therefore, must be exposed for shadow density.

It is essential that you evaluate the scene, especially the shaded areas. Some shaded areas are undoubtedly darker than others. Determine which ones need to show detail on the negative and take the meter reading of such an area.

Exposure for Transparency Film

Transparency (positive) films must generally be exposed for the lighted areas, otherwise highlights look overexposed, become washed out, and lose color saturation. The meter reading therefore must be based on a lighted area.

The above approach of measuring lighted or shaded areas depending on the film in the camera must be used with all meters: reflected, incident, built-in.

Advantage of TTL Metering

A reflected meter reading can be made with a hand-held or a built-in meter. A metering system built into a camera or prism viewfinder has many advantages beyond the fact that you need not carry a separate meter, or have partial or complete exposure automation.

Taking a reading with a separate hand-held meter is a time-consuming process, most impractical in hand-held work. Transferring the information from a meter to the camera can easily cause mistakes.

With a hand-held meter (except a spotmeter), you never know exactly what area you measure. With a built-in meter, the measured area is more clearly or exactly defined on the focusing screen. With the light measured through the lens, the meter reading is automatically adjusted to the area coverage of the lens being used for the picture. When the lens is changed, the measuring angle of the meter also changes. Changes in subject brightness may also be seen while viewing the subject.

The meter reading is also through filters that may be in front of the lens, or close-up accessories such as bellows or tubes between the lens and camera. Thus, the meter automatically compensates for filter and extension factors. With a meter built into the camera, you may also see the lens settings right in the viewfinder and receive all kinds of warning signals indicating that something needs to be done before the picture is taken.

Built-In Metering Methods

To obtain good exposure with a built-in meter, you must know how the built-in meter measures the light. This varies from one camera to another, so study the instruction book. The most common approaches are:

1. Matrix metering where the meter measures different subject areas. A built-in "computer" then figures out a good average. Matrix metering provides the most consistent results in the fully automatic mode, but because you do not know how much each area affects the reading, you really don't know what you are metering.

2. Center weighted means that the metering cell measures the entire subject area seen in the finder, but most of the metering is done in the center. While you do not see the exact area that is measured, you have a fairly clear idea of what part of the subject is or should be measured.

3. Center metering is similar to center weighted but only measures the center of the viewing field, not the edges and corners of the image. The instruction manual should indicate the measuring area.

4. In a spotmeter, built into the camera or hand-held, the exposure is based mainly or only on the spot indicated on the focusing screen. You can point the spot at any area within the subject and you see in the viewfinder the exact area that is measured, including the color and brightness of the area. You know whether you are measuring a lighted or shaded part of the picture. You can also measure different areas of the subject to determine the contrast range. The camera with a built-in spotmeter should never be used in the automatic mode because the spot may measure the wrong area.

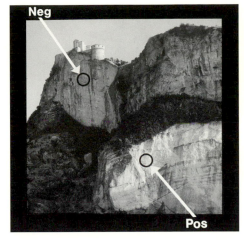

When the subject includes lighted and shaded areas, exposure is different for negative and transparency films. With transparency films (pos), you must expose for an 18% reflectance area in the lighted part of the subject. Negative films (neg) need shadow detail. You must therefore consider the shaded areas when taking a meter reading. Original photo by Josip Ciganovic from Forum 2/87.

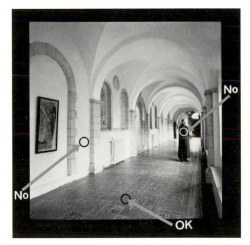

The reflectance values must be considered carefully with a built-in or separate spotmeter. For a correct reading, the spot must be pointed at an 18% reflectance area within the subject. The reading must be adjusted when measuring brighter or darker areas. A spotmeter, however, always shows exactly the area that is measured and should be considered the ultimate metering instrument. Original photo by Mark R. Wallis from Forum 2/88.

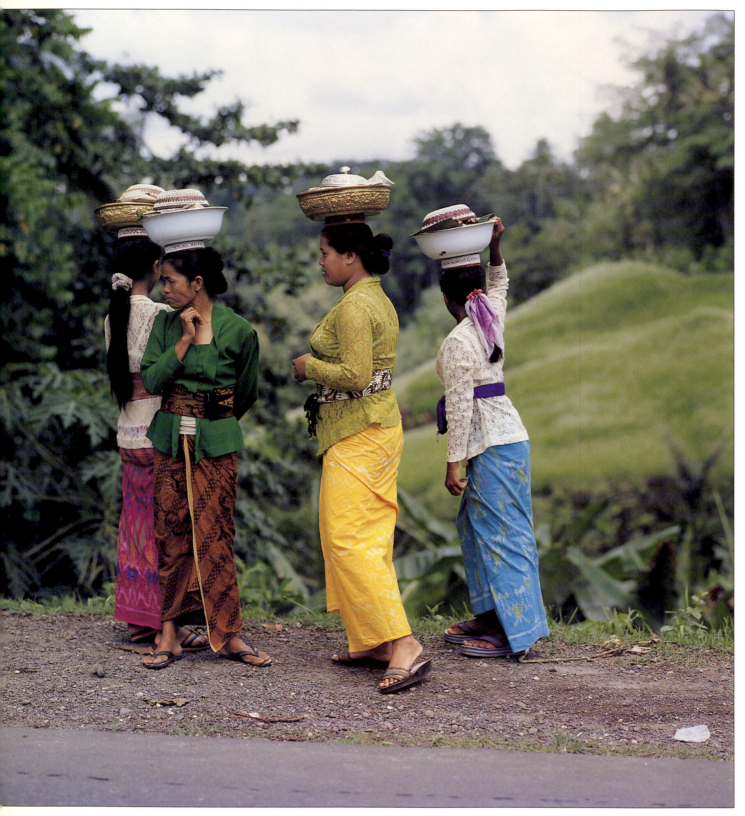

People, especially when they are engaged in activities, should be photographed without a tripod. Insisting on a tripod would make you miss some of the most wonderful picture possibilities. This photo was taken in Bali.

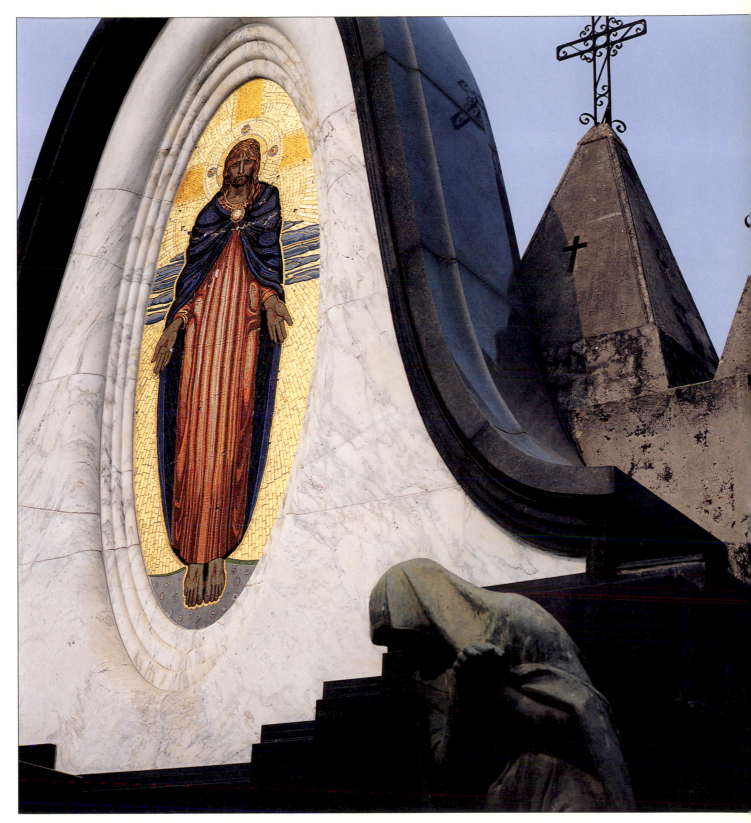

A polarizing filter can eliminate reflections from anything except bare medal when the subject is photographed from an angle. This image was taken with a polarizing filter in a cemetery in Buenos Aires.

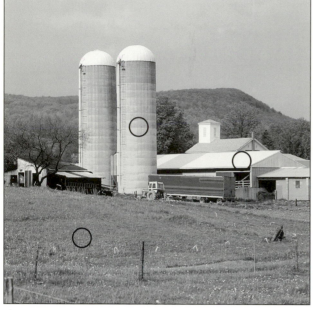

1

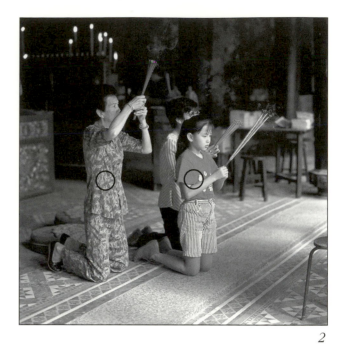

2

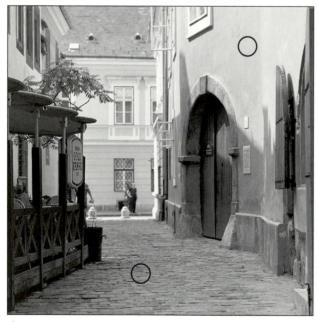

3

4

Four advantages of a spotmeter:
1). You can see and determine accurately what area is measured and select one that reflects 18% of the light (top left).
2). The spotmeter reading is not affected by possible dark or light background areas (top right).
3). The spotmeter makes it easy to measure either lighted or shaded areas or both (bottom left).
4). You can determine all the different brightness values, which is helpful in black and white photography and necessary when working with the zone system (bottom right).

Remember that all built-in metering systems measure the light reflected off the subject. You must consider not only the area that is measured but also the brightness of the area.

Use of Automatic Exposure Cameras

In the majority of picture situations, an automatic matrix or center metering system provides excellent exposures on negative, or even transparency film. In a point & shoot camera, the metering system probably sets everything; the aperture and shutter speed automatically. You may not even know what the settings are.

In other cameras, you can pre-set either the aperture or shutter speed. Only the rest is done automatically. For serious work, you want this type and you definitely want a camera where you can see what the aperture and shutter speed settings are. With such a camera, exposure automation should not be considered just an approach for snapshooting.

Automatic exposure has a definite place in serious photography — a photographer can be instantly and constantly ready to take pictures, capturing images that might have been missed if a meter reading had to be taken first. I love, and would never want to be without, the exposure automation when photographing people on marketplaces, in the streets, in

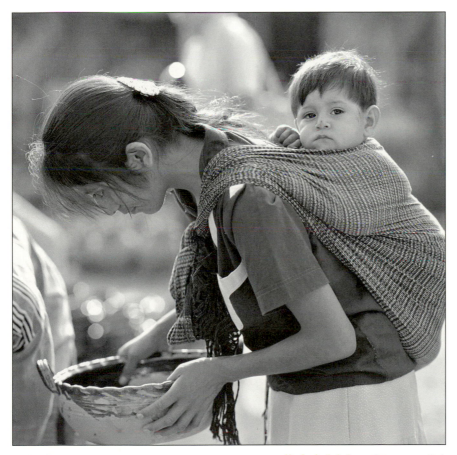

A built-in automatic exposure system is especially helpful for taking candid photographs of people.

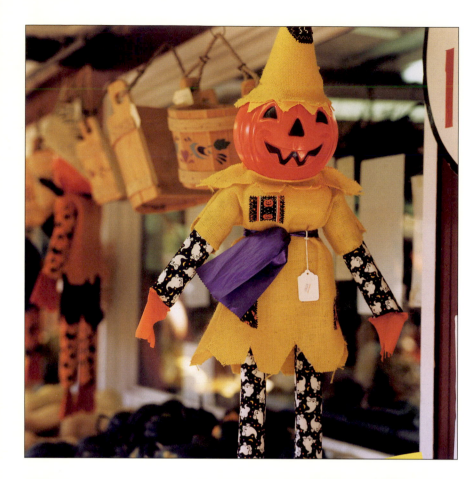

Colors can be changed in developing. For example, developing transparency film, normally done in E 6 (left), as compared to C 41 developer (below).

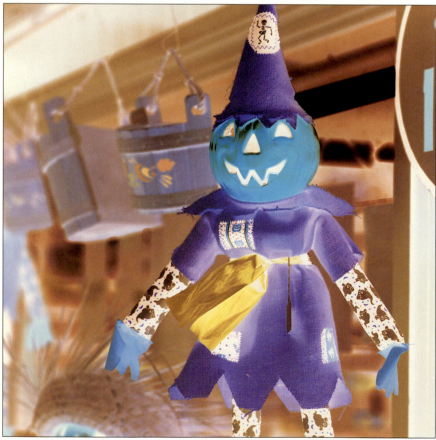

Opposite page: The colors on a boat in Portugal make a beautiful image.

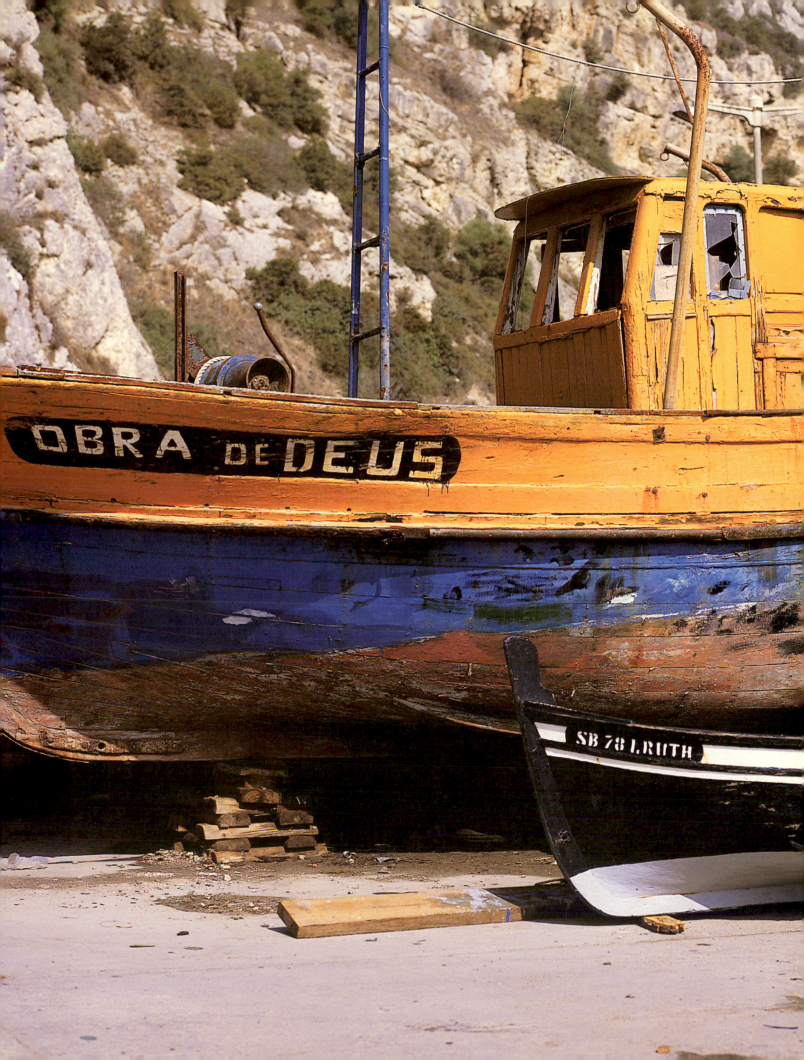

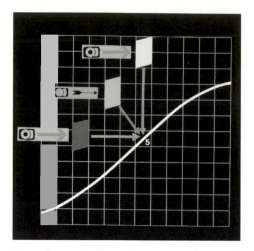

Based on a reflected meter reading, all shades — white, gray and black — will be recorded on the film as a middle grey, in zone 5 (above). To record the different shades properly on the gray scale (below), the reflected meter reading for the brighter shades must be increased, about two stops for white. The readings from the darker shades must be decreased. Incident meter readings do not require this adjustment.

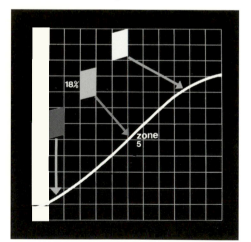

temples, and when making candid photographs of children. The automatic exposure system has often allowed me to record the people on film long before they even realized that they were being photographed.

The important point with any type of automation is for us to determine when the automation has advantages and should therefore be used, and in which cases manual help is needed to accomplish the desired results.

The Zone System

Ansel Adams put the basics of exposure into a system with 10 brightness values (zones) from white to black with a middle tone of 18% reflectance being zone 5. A reflected light meter reading would record any brightness value — white, gray or black — as zone 5.

In black and white photography, we also have the opportunity to change the contrast of the negative by changing exposure and developing times. An increase in exposure of ½ to 1 stop and shortening of the developing time about 20% will produce a lower contrast — a recommended procedure when photographing subjects with a high contrast.

The opposite approach, decreasing the exposure about ½ to 1 stop and lengthening the developing time, is recommended for low contrast subjects such as a landscape in fog. This will increase the contrast on the negative.

Ansel Adams also put this into a system with specific -N and +N values. Following his instructions should produce a normal negative printable on standard grade paper of any subject — with low or high contrast. For details, study a good zone system book.

The zone system cannot be used in color photography as the film developing time cannot be changed to produce higher or lower contrast. The zone idea, however, can be applied. Just as we can place every shade of gray into a zone, we can place every shade of color into a zone.

Any color that reflects 18% becomes a zone value 5. Colors which are one stop brighter are placed in zone 6. Very bright colors that require increasing exposure by 2 stops (like snow) become zone 7. Darker shades that require a 1 or 2 stop decrease become zone 3 or 4. These zone values are indicated at the bottom of the color chart on page 50.

Using zones might make it easier to remember the necessary adjustments in exposure. For example, snow requires a 2 stop increase in exposure based on a reflected light meter reading.

You can easily forget whether exposure needs to be increased or decreased. You are more likely to remember that snow must be placed in zone 7. This approach is especially helpful with a meter that shows zone values. Such a meter also exists built in to a medium format camera.

CHAPTER NINE

Location Flash Photography

Electronic flash is a simple, convenient light source for indoor and outdoor work either to add illumination or to make the lighting more effective and beautiful. Flash photography has become automated, especially in 35mm and the APS format where the flash unit is frequently built into the camera and where flash photography is reduced to one operation — push the button. This is fine for snapshots where you just want to get good exposure without creating any special mood or any special lighting ratio between the flash and existing light. Even as a serious photographer, you may want to use this approach for your family snapshots.

For serious work, on the other hand, you want to control the exposure for the flash and for the existing light. You want to know beforehand what the results will be. To do this, you need a camera that gives you this manual control. Many 35mm's do not. Check the camera specifications carefully. You must then learn how these controls work and how to operate them.

While a flash built into the camera or placed on top of it is fine for many applications, you may also want the option of separating flash and camera or using a second flash unit for better results. These options exist with better 35mm's and with medium format cameras where the flash is always a separate unit. For such more serious work, there are three basic approaches for flash exposure.

Manual Flash

In manual operation, the flash always produces the same amount of light, regardless of how far it is from the subject. As the amount of light is dependent on the distance, the lens aperture must be adjusted to the flash to subject distance. The farther the distance, the larger the aperture must be. There is usually a chart on the flash unit that gives you this information for different film sensitivities so you don't need to make calculations. If you want to make the calculations, keep in mind that everything with light works in the square root of 2. That means if you want to increase the light of any light source the equivalent of one f-stop, you do not move the light to half the distance but only 1.4x closer. The f-stops on your lenses are also based on the same 1.4 number. You can use these figures instead of making distance calculations. If a light is 16 feet from the subject, you move it to 11 feet to get one more stop

"...a simple, convenient light source for indoor and outdoor work..."

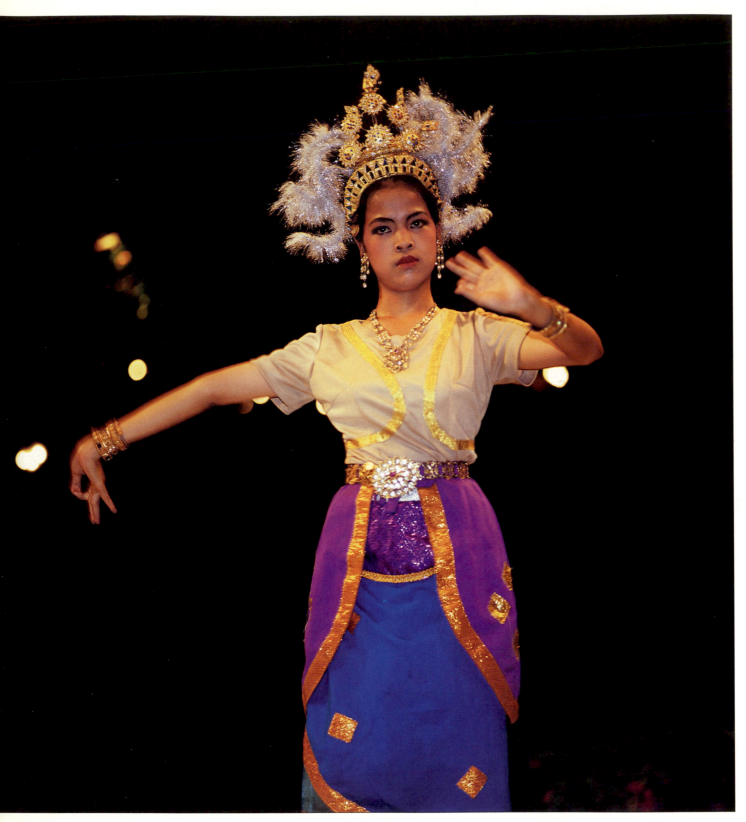

Automatic dedicated flash exposure with a compact flash unit right on the camera. A slow shutter speed of 1/30 sec produced some blur to enhance the feeling that the dancer is moving. ISO 100 film at f/2. This photo was taken in Thailand.

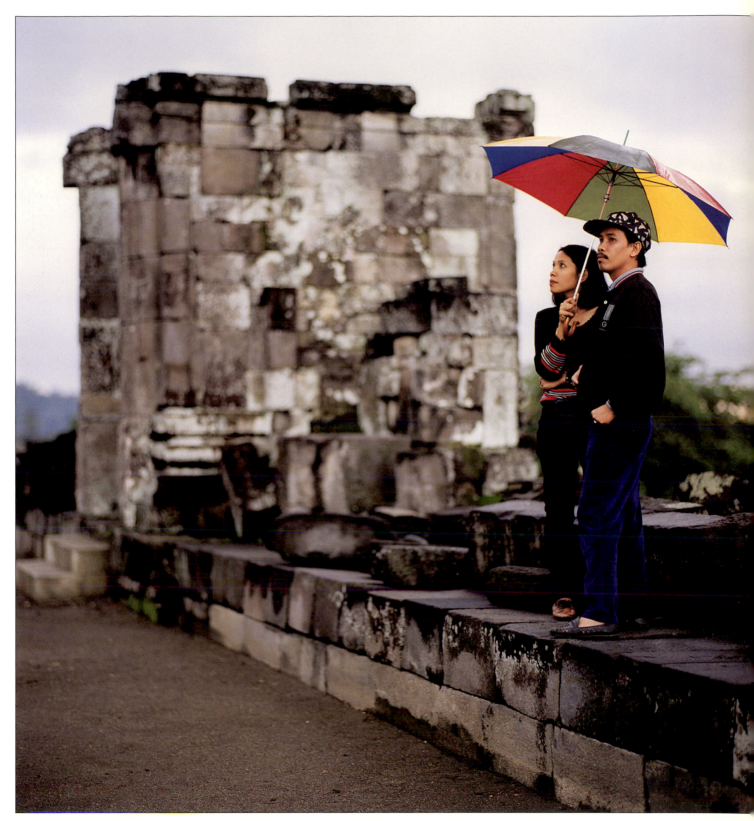

The use of a good lens shade is necessary on any camera and lens to produce images of the best possible contrast, especially when photographing under the white, brilliant skies of overcast, rainy or foggy days.

of light (*f*/16-*f*/11) This also works in meters. Moving the light from 2.8m to 4m reduces the light one *f*-stop. Manual flash is great when the flash is at a fixed distance from the subject, as in studio applications, but will slow you down when the flash is part of the camera or mounted on the camera. Whenever you move closer to or farther from the subject, you must change the aperture. So, manual flash should not be considered for such applications.

Automatic Flash

In the automatic mode, a sensor on the flash unit determines the duration of the flash. The duration is shorter when the flash is close to the subject or the lens is set to a large aperture, and longer when the subject is farther away or a smaller aperture is used. You can therefore move closer to or farther away from the subject without making any changes in the lens aperture. Although you do not know or see what part of the image the sensor measures, automatic flash produces good results in most cases.

The automatic mode allows fast shooting, even from different distances. The film's ISO is set on the flash unit. Most units have an adjustment for reducing the flash illumination to ½, ¼ or even further.

Dedicated Flash

The modern location flash approach is known as "dedicated." The flash is electronically coupled to the camera with the light measured by a sensor in the camera. The flash unit may be part of the camera or separate (as in the medium format). If the separate flash unit is not or cannot be electronically coupled to the camera, the flash can still be used in either the automatic or manual mode.

A dedicated system is completely automatic in some cameras without giving you any option for control. In others, you maintain control over all the lens and camera settings and the resulting exposure. You can select the aperture and shutter speed that produces the desired depth of field and the desired exposure for the existing light. You probably also have the possibility of controlling the flash exposure. For serious and professional location flash photography, you must select a camera that gives you full control of aperture and shutter speed and also allows you to control the flash exposure.

Advantages of Dedicated Flash

Both automatic and dedicated flash give you the freedom to move around, photographing from different distances without worrying about aperture adjustments. This approach allows you to capture action instantly and with consistently good exposures, both indoors (where flash may be the main light) or outdoors (where flash is used to fill in shaded areas). The dedicated mode has many additional advantages that really make it the modern location flash approach. Exposures are amazingly accurate and consistent because they are based on the light that actually falls on the film. The light is also measured through the lens. The measuring area is thus directly related to the area coverage of each lens. The flash ready light is visible in the camera's viewfinder. You can keep your eye constantly in the finder and never lose contact with your subject.

Dedicated flash gives you the peace of knowing that exposures are correct because an exposure signal shows whether the film received sufficient light. This signal is also visible in the camera's viewfinder.

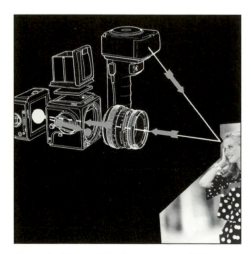

In a dedicated flash system in 35mm or medium format cameras, a sensor in the camera measures the light reflected off the film plane and turns off the flash when it has received the proper amount of light. The light is also measured through the lens and the ready light is visible in the viewfinder.

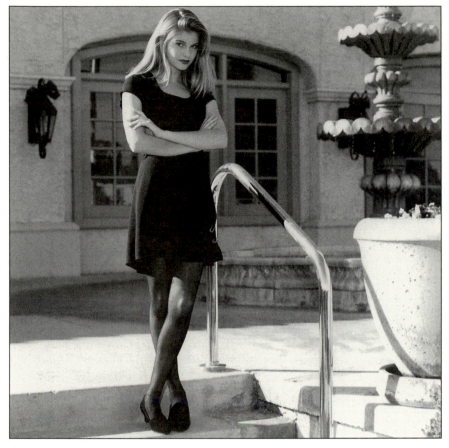

Dedicated flash provides surprisingly accurate exposures while giving you the freedom of changing the flash to subject distance without any changes in the lens setting.

A dedicated system also reduces the danger of making mistakes, such as shooting at a shutter speed that is not synchronized for flash. There are usually warning signals or controls in the camera to minimize this possibility. A good dedicated system will also offer simple solutions for changing the flash exposure in fractions of f-stops.

Dedicated flash units made specifically for a camera system are electronically dedicated to the camera need or have no adjustments. Other flash units are dedicated by setting them to TTL. That bypasses all settings on the flash, including the ISO which is set on the camera.

Any shutter speed that synchronizes for flash produces the proper exposures for the flash lit subject, but it may not produce the most effective image. It does not consider the amount of existing light in the room or the brightness of the daylight outdoors. You want this existing light part of your picture.

Making the Existing Light Part of the Picture

All location flash photography — indoors or out — is done in existing light — daylight outdoors, daylight or interior lighting indoors. Outdoor pictures and many flash pictures indoors are more effective and look more natural when the existing light is part of the image — if you can see the location instead of the people being surrounded by darkness. The electronic flash is then used to augment the existing lighting.

"You want to make this existing light part of your picture."

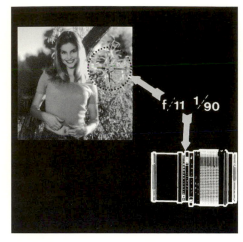

f/11 1/90

To balance the existing light with flash, take a meter reading of the existing light, the daylight, and the background in a portrait. Then make the lens settings accordingly (above). The flash exposure is automatic (right).

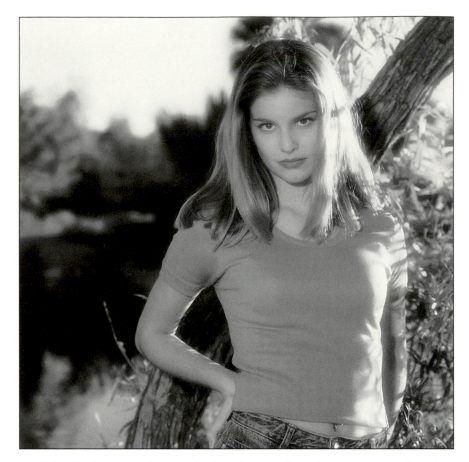

"You can do your location flash work with a more compact, lighter unit..."

It is simple to produce such flash images, but the shutter speed setting needs attention. The shutter speed determines to what extent the existing light becomes part of the picture.

Start by measuring the daylight, or the room light, using your usual metering method with a built-in or a separate hand-held meter. Then decide whether the background should be recorded as it is, brighter, or darker, and use the meter reading to produce the desired results.

If you set the aperture and shutter speed as shown on the meter, the background will be recorded at the "normal" level. You can make it darker by selecting a shorter shutter speed, lighter by setting to a longer shutter speed (without changing the aperture). When using a focal plane shutter, the shutter speed must not be shorter than specified in the instruction book. A lens shutter synchronizing for flash at all shutter speeds has a definite advantage, especially in medium format cameras where focal plane flash sync may be limited to speeds up to 1/60 sec or even 1/30 sec.

In bright sunlight, it is often desirable or necessary to shoot at 1/250 or even 1/500 sec. The high shutter speed allows you to use a larger aperture which in turn requires less power from the flash. You can do your location flash work with a more compact, lighter unit, and you get many more flashes from one battery charge.

Flash Exposure

The flash exposure determined by the sensor in the camera produces the desired results in many situations, especially indoors where the flash is usually the main light.

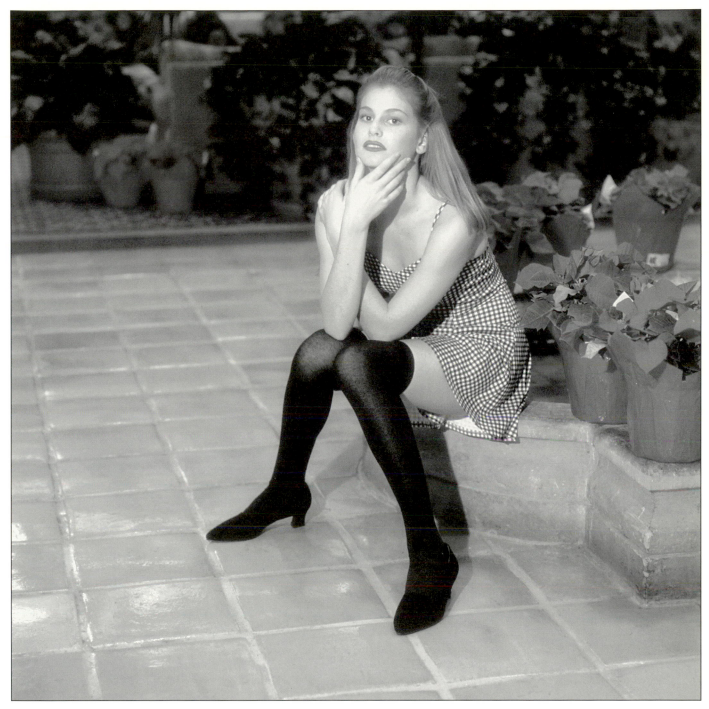

Indoor portraits, with the exposure based on existing light, can be improved tremendously by adding flash without becoming aware of the flash. The indoor light is still the main light, which is the way many indoor flash pictures should look.

In other situations, particularly outdoors where the flash is meant to fill in the shaded areas with the sunlight remaining the main light source, a reduction in the flash exposure will more likely produce a more natural image — with the sunlight being brighter than the flash fill. The use of flash is hardly noticeable. For this purpose, you need a camera that offers this adjustment to at least -2 f-stops. The adjustment is usually made electronically by programming a flash fill value in fractions of f-stops into the camera. To determine the best value for your type of photography, it is best to make a film test with your camera and your film and have the film processed in your laboratory. In place of a film test, I suggest the following:

For outdoor portraits, in the diffused light of an overcast day, or on a sunny day (with the sunlight used as a back or side light), reduce the flash to -1½ to -2. When flash is the main light, you usually do not reduce the flash unless the picture is made in a very bright room.

On some medium format cameras without a built-in meter, the reduction in the flash exposure is made by increasing the flash ISO setting (on the camera). If you set the ISO to 200 for 100 ISO film, the flash exposure is reduced one f-stop. With automatic flash, the adjustment is made the same way, increasing the ISO setting on the automatic flash unit.

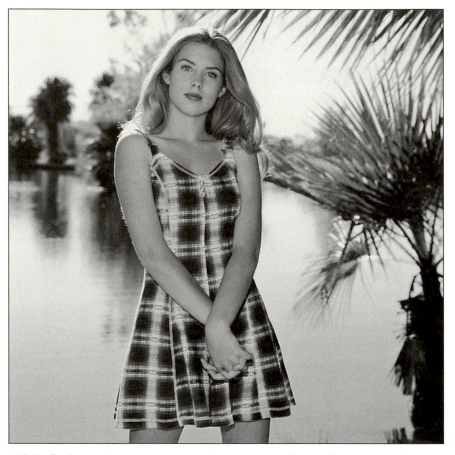

While flash can improve any outdoor portrait, the results are usually most effective in sunlight, used either as a sidelight or a backlight. The photo above is an example of sunlight used as a backlight.

Subject Brightness

While dedicated and automatic flash produce good exposures in most situations, be aware that they can produce perfect results only if the subject that reflects the light to the sensor has an 18% reflectance value — a medium shade of color. A bright subject reflects more light to the sensor and shortens the flash duration, causing underexposure. You can compensate for this by setting the flash fill function to a plus value or setting the ISO dial to a lower setting (ISO 50 for ISO 100 film lengthens the flash duration). In practical photography, the differences seldom exceed more than ⅔ f-stops, not really

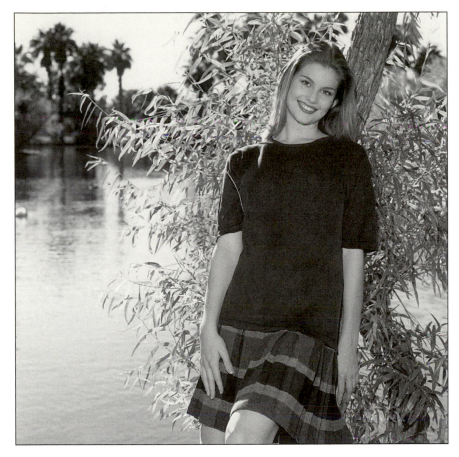

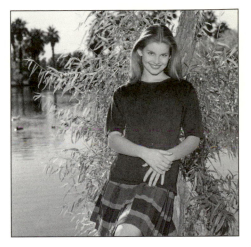

Outdoor portraits look more natural when the flash exposure is reduced, which is possible on better 35mm and medium format cameras. In the photo above, the flash was reduced the equivalent of ⅓ f-stop which still looks bright. A reduction of 1½ f-stops, pictured on the left, looks more like a fill light and is more natural-looking.

enough to be concerned with negative film. This is true even in a wedding photograph with a bride dressed in white. Here, most images probably include not only white but other shades, flowers, flesh tones or the groom's black tuxedo as well.

Film Reflectance

In a dedicated flash system, the sensor measures the light reflected off the film emulsion. The sensor must be matched to the reflectance of the film. There are reflectance differences among the films which are usually not pointed out to the photographer. The differences are not too great (especially among transparency films) and rarely exceed ⅔ of a stop with negative emulsions reflecting more light, causing slight underexposure. The range exceeds with special films like Polaroid, for example.

I suggest that you make your own film tests with your dedicated flash system. Photograph a subject, preferably with 18% reflectance on your type of film, and have the film processed in your lab. Underexposure can be corrected by setting the flash fill fraction to a + value, the ISO to a lower value. When making the film test, make certain that the entire subject area measured by the sensor has the same reflectance, preferably 18%.

Producing Better Flash Illumination

The flash head on portable flash units is small, producing a very directional harsh light with sharply outlined shadow lines. Placing a diffusion filter over the flash head only reduces the amount of light, but does not produce a softer light. To produce a softer light in the studio or on location, you

"…make your own film tests with your dedicated flash system."

must increase the size of the light source so the light hits the subject from somewhat different angles. Soft boxes accomplish such soft lighting beautifully in the studio, and of course on location.

For professional work, such as fashion photography on location, you may also want to use a professional soft box. For most location work, where you must be mobile, you can add a small softbox over the flash head of a portable unit. Such units are available from various companies in sizes about 5-7 inches and are usable with most flash heads. Adding the box reduces the light somewhat, but this is more than compensated by the beautiful results. The portraits no longer look like flash snapshots but have softer, perhaps almost invisible shadow lines.

Some photographers accomplish similar results with reflected flash. The flash head is pointed upwards towards a white reflecting bouncer attached to the flash. The reflector, which must be larger than the flash head, then bounces the light into the subject. I found the use of a small softbox more practical.

Color of Light & Flash

When combining flash with existing light, you must also pay attention to the color of both light sources. You want to match the two light sources as closely as possible. There is no problem during regular daylight hours, as electronic flash has about the same color temperature as noontime sunlight. If you use flash as a fill light early in the morning or late afternoon, the flash fill will be too blue and cold compared to the warm sunlight.

Place a warming filter over the flash unit. A filter such as 81B or 81C should help. Gelatin filters are good for this purpose. You do not need a quality filter since the filter is used only to change the color of the light. You do not take a picture through the filter.

Multiple Flash

If flash is used as fill light, a flash unit on the camera produces excellent results. Used as a main light, you can produce more professional results by using two flash heads — a main light and a fill as you would in a studio set-up. Also, like in a studio, the main light is a side or ¾ light, and the fill light can come right from the camera.

Both flash units must fire simultaneously. This can be accomplished with wires, or in a more professional and practical way with slave units. The flash on the camera then fires the remote main light by means of infrared or radio signals.

The main light on the side can be used in the manual mode — setting it at the distance based on the lens aperture, or in the automatic fashion — so you need not worry about the distance. The fill light on or near the camera should be in the automatic or dedicated mode. It is fired from the flash sync contact on the camera or lens. The fill light should be reduced at least the equivalent of one f-stop, probably even more. You do this with the flash fill function or the ISO setting, depending on the system or mode you are using.

Flash Applications

Flash can improve location photography not only when photographing people. The addition of flash can improve any pictures taken on location with poor or unknown lighting. For example, fluorescent lights do not produce good colors. Flash, which is matched to daylight color film, can help to

"...you can produce more professional results by using two flash heads..."

produce more pleasing colors, especially flesh tones. The flash is then an addition to the fluorescent light, not a replacement — and not necessarily used to light the entire room, only the people in the room. Take a normal meter reading of the existing light as usual and set aperture and shutter speed accordingly. To reduce the effect of the fluorescent illumination, change to a shorter shutter speed: perhaps to 1/60 second or even 1/125 if the meter indicates 1/30 second.

Flash has a wonderful application in nature photography. When the sky is overcast, producing flat lighting, flash can add contrast and produce lighted and shaded areas, making your nature shots look as if they were taken in sunlight.

Wooded areas may be in complete shade even on a sunny day, resulting in long exposures — frequently associated with a blue color cast typical when photographing in shaded areas. Flash eliminates all problems and simplifies the photography by allowing a shorter shutter speed. The short flash duration also reduces the danger of camera or subject movement showing up on your pictures. Even when the lighting is fairly decent, flash has the advantage of giving you complete control over the lighting. You can place the flash unit so it produces a front, side, back or overhead light without having to wait for the sun to move to the proper spot.

Indoor Flash Photography

When using portable flash indoors, I recommend that you consider the existing light in the room whenever possible, instead of taking such pictures at any aperture or shutter speed combination that might seem practical. This approach will, in many cases, reward you with more effective flash pictures where the room is part of the photo instead of the people being surrounded in darkness. This approach can be especially useful in social functions, such as weddings, which are frequently held in beautifully decorated rooms.

Basically, we are using the same approach as we do in an outdoor portrait where we set the aperture and shutter speed to record the surrounding area and background with the proper exposure. When shooting indoors, take a meter reading of the existing light (daylight, tungsten) in the room, then try to use a aperture/shutter speed combination that provides the proper exposure for the existing light or something close to it.

Obviously, since the amount of existing light in the room is limited, your possibilities are also limited as you need to work at shutter speeds short enough for hand-held work of moving subjects. Even an aperture/shutter speed combination that is one or two stops less than necessary for the room makes the background still visible and is better than taking all the pictures automatically at 1/125 sec. A one stop underexposure may even be preferable. Inside a church, for example, you may want to put the camera on a tripod for some overall shots.

Using a faster film, such as 400 ISO, instead of 100, gives you much more leeway and at the same time may allow you to work with a more compact flash unit. Do not hesitate to use fairly slow shutter speeds, such as 1/30 or 1/60 sec, with flash. The flash duration is short, eliminating the danger of unsharpness due to camera motion, at least in the flashlit subjects.

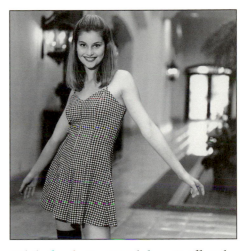

While the shutter speed doesn't affect the flash exposure, it does determine the exposure for the existing light. A slower shutter speed, 1/15 sec (above) for example, makes the room part of the picture. A shorter shutter speed of 1/60 sec (below) keeps the room dark. The dedicated flash exposure is the same.

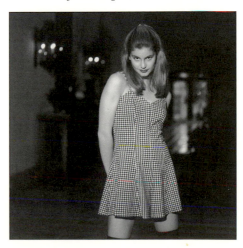

"...designed to produce good image quality at close distances."

Chapter Ten

Close-up Photography

Lenses focus down to a certain minimum distance. Macro lenses are available for many 35mm cameras. They are operated like "ordinary" lenses but focus much closer, usually down to inches. They simplify close-up photography as most or all work can be done without adding accessories. These lenses are usually optically designed to provide good image quality at close distances.

Non-macro lenses on 35mm or medium format cameras allow taking pictures below their minimum distance with the use of accessories. That does not necessarily complicate close-up photography, but you must know the accessories, what they do and how they must be used.

Magnification

Everything in close-up photography revolves around magnification: the relationship between the size of the actual subject and the size of the image as recorded on the film or seen on the focusing screen. As the size of the subject is usually known in close-up photography, magnification can be determined quickly — even before you set up the camera — by relating the subject size to the negative size. The latter is 24x36mm in 35mm, 55x55mm for a 6x6 square format medium format camera. If the subject is about the same size as the negative, we have 1:1 or lifesize magnification. If the subject is twice as large, we must bring it down to half its size which means 0.5x or 1:2 magnification. If the subject is only about half the size of the film format, we enlarge it and have 2x or 2:1 magnification.

Close-up Lenses

For low magnification work, when you wish to go just below the minimum focusing distance of the lens (for example, to focus down to two feet when the lens only permits focusing to three feet), close-up lenses are the easiest to use. They are mounted on the front of the lens like a filter, and can therefore be attached, changed or removed quickly and easily. They do not require an increase in exposure and they can be used on any type and focal length of lens, on zoom or fixed focal length lenses.

The power of close-up lenses is frequently indicated in diopters like eyeglasses, +1; +2; +3 diopters. Diopter is another way of expressing the focal

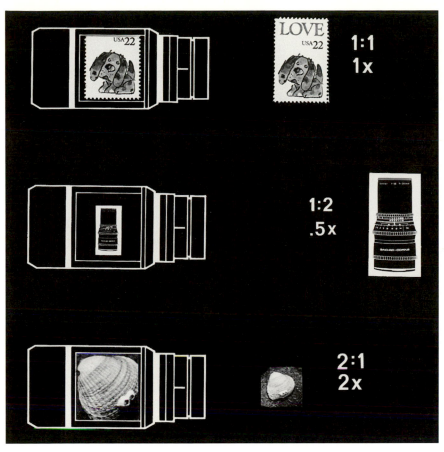

Magnification is the ratio in size between the actual subject and its size on the focusing screen or film. If the image is half the size of the subject, we have a 0.5x (or 1:2) magnification. A 2x (or 2:1) magnification exists when the image is twice the size of the subject.

length of a lens or system. 1 diopter equals a 1 meter focal length (39⅓ inches), 2 diopters is ½ meter or 19½ inches. A ½ diopter lens has a focal length of 2 meters (79 inches).

This is worth knowing because there is a direct optical relationship between the focal length of a close-up lens and focusing distance. If any lens on any camera is set at infinity, a close-up lens produces a sharp image on the film when the distance from the close-up lens to the subject is equal to the focal length of the close-up lens — 1 meter or 39⅓ inches for a 1 diopter lens. You can obtain a sharp image at closer distances by turning the focusing ring to closer distances.

To go just below the minimum focusing distance with any lens, select a close-up lens with a focal length roughly equal to the minimum focusing distance. To be more specific:

- For lenses with a minimum focusing distance of 5 feet or longer, select a 2 meter focal length (0. 5 diopters).

- For lenses with a minimum focusing distance of around 3 feet, select the 1 meter focal length (1 diopter).

- For lenses with a minimum focusing distance of 2 feet or less, select the 0. 5 meter (2 diopters).

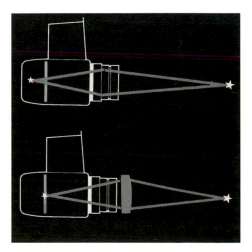

A subject closer than the minimum focusing distance of the lens forms its image behind the film plane (top camera). A proxar or close-up lens in front of the camera lens can bring the image on the film plane (bottom camera).

73

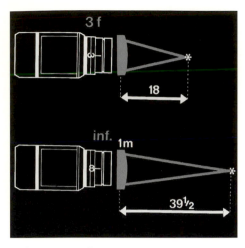

When any lens on any camera is focused to infinity, the distance from the close-up lens to the subject is equal to the focal length of the close-up lens, or 1 meter (or 39½ inches) for a one diopter lens (bottom camera). You can take pictures closer by turning the focusing ring on the lens to a closer distance than infinity (top camera).

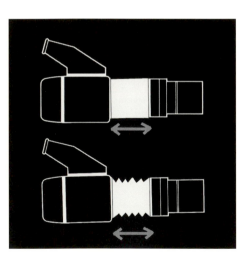

For higher magnification, the lens must be moved farther from the film plane. This can be done with extension tubes (top camera) or with bellows (bottom camera). A bellows extension equal to the length of an extension tube creates the same image on the film.

The closer you want to go, the stronger the close-up lens needs to be (higher diopter value). You can combine two Proxar lenses. The power of the combination is obtained by adding the two diopter strengths: a +1 and a +2 diopter lens yields a +3, for example. Proxar lenses decrease the image quality, especially at the edges.

The stronger the lens, the more noticeable the loss of sharpness. With lenses up to two diopters, the loss is usually not objectionable or even noticeable when the lens aperture is closed two to three *f*-stops. Image quality suffers with stronger lenses (3 or more diopters) and therefore, I do not recommend them for critical work.

Higher Magnification Work

For higher magnification work, consider extension tubes or bellows. Both mount between camera and lens and both perform the same function. They allow you to move the lens further away from the film plane.

In a way, these accessories extend the focusing range of a lens. A bellows extended to the same length as a tube produces the same image with the same lens. Which one should you choose? Here are a few points to consider:

1. Extension tubes are more compact and easier to carry.

2. Tubes should be considered when the required extension is low. Bellows should be considered for longer extensions.

3. Extension tubes are solid pieces and are able to support any lens including long, heavy telephotos.

4. Good bellows have two adjusting knobs, one for changing subject distance, the other for changing image distance. This simplifies and speeds up close-up photography. Bellows should be considered for extensive close-up work.

5. A transparency copy holder can be attached to the front of some bellows for simple slide copying.

Length of Tube or Bellows Extension

The area coverage is always determined by the focal length of the lens in relation to the length of the tube or bellows.

To cover a smaller area, you can:

(a) Change to a longer tube or increase the extension of the bellows with the same lens, or

(b) Change to a shorter focal length lens and use the same tube or bellows extension.

(In either case you will also need to move the camera closer to the subject.)

Exposure

Since extension tubes and bellows move the lens farther away from the film plane, exposure must be increased. If the meter reading is taken with a meter in the camera that measures the light through the lens (TTL) there is no need to consider the increase, since the light is also metered through the accessories. If the meter reading is taken with a separate meter, the exposure must be increased.

Correct *f* value = *f* value from meter x focal length of lens ÷ focal length of lens + extension. (the focal length and the extension length must be in the same units, mm for example).

$$\text{Aperture value} \quad = \quad \frac{\text{aperture on meter x focal length}}{\text{focal length + extension}}$$

Example for *f*/11, 50mm focal length and 50mm extension:

$$= \quad \frac{11 \times 50}{50 + 50} = \quad \frac{550}{100} \quad = \quad 5.5$$

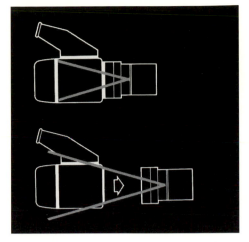

Whenever a lens is moved away from the film plane, exposure must be increased as the light is spread over a larger area.

Depth of Field with Different Lenses & Close-Up Accessories

Contrary to general belief, depth of field is not affected or determined by the close-up accessory. In practical close-up photography, where you normally want to photograph an area of a specific size, depth of field is again unaffected by the focal length of the lens. Depth of field is determined solely by the area of coverage (magnification) and the lens aperture. For example, at life-size magnification the depth of field at *f*/11 is about 2mm with any lens or accessory. The only way to increase the depth of field is to stop the lens down further, if this is possible, or cover a larger area and crop out the desired area later. Closing the aperture down two stops will approximately double the depth of field.

Depth of Field at Various Magnifications

Magnification	Total Depth of Field in mm at *f*/11	
	A	B
0. 1x	100	50
0. 2x	30	15
0. 3x	15	7
0. 5x	6	3
0. 8x	3	1½
1x	2	1

A is for general work
B is for work where critical sharpness is important.

Photographing Subjects Life-Size

To obtain life-size magnification with any lens, you can add an extension tube or use a bellows extension equal to the focal length of the lens. The distance from the subject to the film plane is then equal to 4 times the focal length of the lens, and is equally divided between the front and the rear. Life-size magnification with a 6x4.5cm camera means covering an area 55x40mm. In 35mm, 1:1 means covering a smaller 24x36mm area. Covering the same 24x36mm area with a 6x4.5cm camera means a higher magnification of about 1.7x with consequently less depth of field. This is the basic explanation of why depth of field in the medium format is shallower than in 35mm.

Photographing Close-ups

The use of a tripod is highly recommended for various reasons. Depth of field is shallow, so focusing must be accurate. A slight change in camera position can change the composition or background drastically. In close-up work, backgrounds must be carefully evaluated. Since small apertures are usually called for, shutter speeds may be relatively long. Since close-up photography frequently means low angle photography, a tripod designed for this purpose may have to be considered. A type with a reversible center post may be the solution.

Don't forget about hand-held close-up photography. It can be done with macro lenses or any close-up accessories and can be practical especially for low angle work. Lying on the ground, resting on your elbows, makes a beautiful camera support.

In hand-held work, automatic focusing is a definite benefit. In the manual approach, do not attempt to focus by turning the focusing ring. You will be more successful if you pre-set the focusing ring on the lens or the extension on a bellows, then move the camera until the desired part of the subject appears sharp on the focusing screen.

Lighting

The existing lighting is frequently not effective for close-up work. The subject may be in complete or partial shade, the sun may not be in the right position, or it may be an overcast day resulting in a flat image without shaded and lighted areas.

Try to improve the light. Many nature photographers use mirrors. Properly placed, they can reflect sunlight into shaded areas. Mirrors can improve the lighting but you are still limited in the choice of aperture and shutter speed and mirrors must be moved as the sun changes position.

Electronic flash is a better choice. The light from the electronic flash unit can be made to fill shaded areas, or it can become the main light when photographing on an overcast day or in complete shade. If so, take the flash off the camera. Make the flash a side, ¾ or backlight.

Place the light where it produces the most effective image. You can also use more than one flash unit or combine the flash with a reflector as you might do in a studio.

A dedicated flash system, measuring the light through the lens and close-up accessory, will in many cases provide the correct exposure automatically. However, since we are combining flash with daylight and the combination of the two lights determines the effectiveness of the final image, a test exposure (on Polaroid, if possible) is recommended. In any case, you must consider the daylight, so start by taking a meter reading of an important area — the background perhaps — and set aperture and shutter speed

"The use of a tripod is highly recommended..."

accordingly. If you want to make the background lighter or darker to produce the most effective close-up, shorten or lengthen the shutter speed.

High Magnification Photography

With the close-up accessories discussed so far, you can obtain magnifications up to about 2x, which means covering an area about 12x18mm in 35mm, 27x27mm for the square medium format.

You may be able to obtain higher magnifications in one of two ways without getting involved in photomicroscopy. Some 35mm lenses are designed to be used in the reversed fashion, which means mounting them on the camera with the front towards the film plane and camera. Investigate the options and obtain the instructions from the manufacturer.

A few companies make special lenses for high magnification work. They look like objectives for a microscope and come from the microscope division of the optical company. These objectives are used in front of a bellows with a special adapter. The bellows extension is used for focusing. The length of the bellows extension also determines the magnification, so a wide range of magnifications can be obtained with the same lens. Such lenses are most likely available from camera companies that also manufacture optical instruments, especially microscopes. Contact the manufacturer for details.

High magnification work, covering areas ½ or ¼ inch in size (5 to 12mm) is fascinating as such images reveal details that we normally don't see. I have used such lenses to photograph details in postage stamps and the color patterns in fall leaves. They have also been used to produce the 10x blow-ups from negatives and transparencies published in this book.

"A few companies make special lenses for high magnification work."

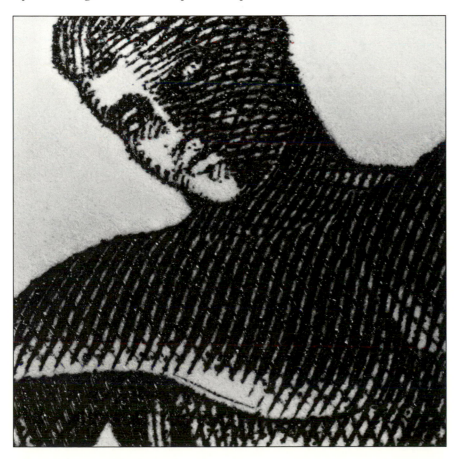

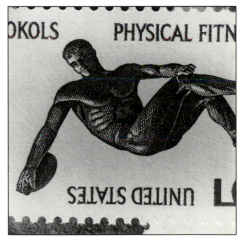

High magnification images, such as a small part out of a postage stamp, can be obtained by reversing lenses, if this is possible, or by using special high magnification lenses in combination with a bellows and an adapter to hold these lenses. These lenses are usually equipped with a microscope thread. Such a lens was used in this example on a 6x6cm medium format camera.

CHAPTER ELEVEN

Filters for Better Image Quality & Effect

"...to produce a better or more effective image..."

There are basically two reasons for using filters — to produce a better or more effective image and to add a special effect to the image. Special effect filters allow you to change colors, surround the highlights with streaks or stars, add a blur or fog, or produce multiple images, *et cetera*. They serve a good purpose in amateur and professional photography. My main reason for using filters is to produce technically better images.

Filters in Black & White Photography

Color filters are helpful in black and white photography. They darken or lighten subject areas of certain colors. Thus, they enhance the contrast and emphasize or suppress other areas that are of a different color. Use the color wheel to determine how different color filters change gray tones.

A filter of a certain color always transmits the light of that particular color. Red, for example, transmits red, thus making subjects of that color appear lighter in the print. The filter darkens subjects that have the color from the opposite side of the color wheel (blue in the case of a yellow filter).

Neutral Density Filters

Neutral density filters, also called gray filters, are used in both black and white and color photography. Made from neutral gray-colored glass, the

Density	Percentage Light Transmission	Increase in Exposure in Exposure Values or f-stops
0. 3	50	1
0. 6	25	2
0. 9	12	3

neutral density filter is designed to reduce the amount of light reaching the film without changing the tonal rendition of various colors.

Neutral density filters are most helpful outdoors when the light is too bright to permit photography at large apertures, to produce shallow depth of field, or allow slow shutter speeds for blurred motion or zoom effects. Neutral density filters come in different densities; the most common ones are listed in the chart on page 78.

Light Balance & Conversion Filters

Light balance and conversion filters are used in color photography for matching the color quality of the illumination to that of the film. This is necessary when subjects, flesh tones or products, for example, must be recorded in their true color under any light source.

Matching color is seldom necessary for landscape photography even when photographed in the warm early morning or late afternoon sunlight. Landscapes are usually photographed at these daylight times because the warm light adds a special touch and mood to the scene. Don't destroy the effect by trying to change the color to match the noontime sunlight.

Light balance and skylight filters have been recommended for outdoor photography on overcast, foggy or rainy days when the color temperature is unknown and is usually higher than sunlight, producing a bluish cast. They were also recommended when photographing into shaded areas on a sunny day. The light in the shade is actually the reflected blue skylight and renders shaded areas with a blue cast.

I have found that this is no longer necessary with most color films today. The tendency for a bluish cast has been reduced. It is no longer objectionable or even visible, especially with the latest special transparency films deigned to produce a warmer rendition. These slide films are designated with X or W. I have not used any warming filters for my slide photography for at least seven years.

Haze, UV & Skylight Filters

Haze and UV (ultraviolet) filters do not change colors to a noticeable degree. They absorb UV rays. Most modern lenses, however, have lens elements made from glass that also absorbs UV light and often to a higher degree than a UV filter. Consequently, these filters do not improve pictures to any noticeable degree. UV filters also do not improve distant shots.

While haze and UV filter do not improve image quality, I recommend their use for lens protection.

Lenses are the most expensive components in a camera system. They are also the components that are most easily damaged and probably the most expensive to repair.

A simple way to protect the front element is with an optically plain piece of glass, which is easy to clean and relatively cheap to replace. A skylight, UV, or haze filter can serve this purpose.

Each of your lenses should be equipped with a filter. It is much too time-consuming to be switching filters from one lens to another every time you change lenses.

Each filter should be of the highest quality as it becomes a part of the lens. For color photography, use the same filter made by the same company on every lens to avoid possible differences in color rendition.

"...warm light adds a special touch and mood to the scene."

"...improve distant shots by eliminating the haze..."

Polarizing Filters — Applications

Polarizing filters can improve outdoor photos in various ways:

1. The filters can darken skies (especially blue skies) and make them more dramatic on any type of film — color or black and white. This is possible only with sidelight (the sun shining from the side).

2. Polarizing filters can improve distant shots by eliminating the haze and bluish cast. The use of such a filter can make a dramatic difference in the quality of such pictures. Again, it works only with sidelight.

3. The filters can increase the color saturation of many outdoor subjects by eliminating or reducing reflections on the surface of the subject.

4. The filters can eliminate reflections on shiny surfaces such as store windows, murals, *et cetera*. This happens only if the subject is photographed from an angle of 30 to 40 degrees.

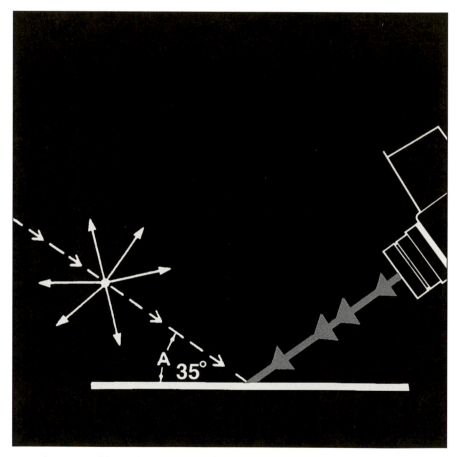

A polarizing filter eliminates reflections only when the subject is photographed from an angle between 30 and 40 degrees, depending on the material (glass, water, et cetera).

5. The filters can eliminate reflections from water surfaces which may or may not be desirable. Reflections make water surfaces beautiful and give them life. Use your judgment while viewing the scene with

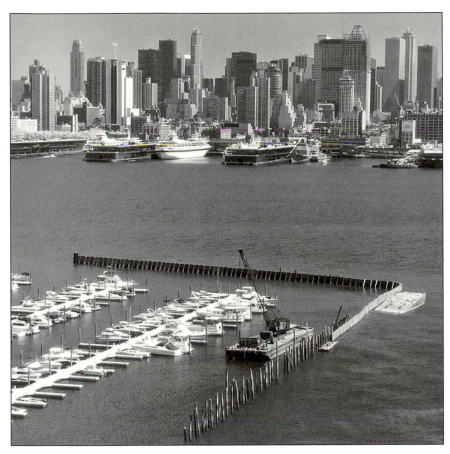

A polarizing filter can improve distance shots, but only in sidelight.

and without the filter. Reflections can be eliminated only when photographing the water surface from an angle.

6. Polarization is very helpful for copying.

Polarization in Copying

Copying results can be improved dramatically with polarization. Since the subject, the copy page, painting, photographs, *et cetera*, must be photographed straight on (90 degrees) to avoid keystoning, a polarizing filter over the camera lens is not enough.

The light that reaches the copy (tungsten or electronic flash) must be polarized. Polarizing filters must be placed over the light source or light sources. The filter over the lens is then rotated for what is known as cross polarization. If more than one light is used, the filter over each light source must be rotated in the same direction.

This can be checked by placing the filters on top of each other. They are polarized in the same direction when you see the brightest image through the filters.

When using flash (other than a studio type with modeling light), place some kind of a continuous light source (a regular lamp) next to the flash but also behind a polarizing filter. The continuous light is necessary to study the effect on the focusing screen while rotating the filter on the camera lens.

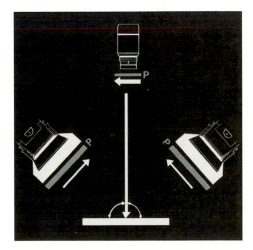

A copying set-up consists of the camera with a polarizing filter over the camera lens, and one or two light sources (flash or tungsten), with polarizing filters over each light source.

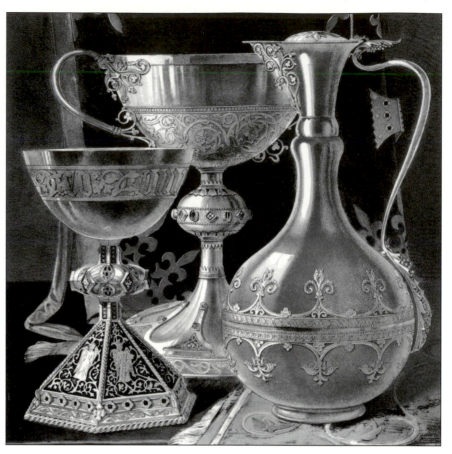

Copying with polarizing filters over the lens and light sources eliminates reflections and improves the color or black and white photographs of any document, painting, book page, or cover.

> "Neutral density filters can be used to darken some areas..."

Partial Filtering

Filters can be positioned in front of the lens so only part of the image receives filtered light. Neutral-density filters can be used to darken some areas, color filters to change colors in some areas, while others are unfiltered. Special filters that are clear over half of their area, and neutral gray or colored over the other half, are readily available — especially in the square shape.

When positioning the filter, you must view the ground-glass image at the aperture that will be used. Or, even better, determine the aperture that produces the desired results while manually opening and closing the diaphragm. You will find that the position of the dividing line changes as the diaphragm is closed down and that the sharpness of the dividing line between the filtered and non-filtered area depends on the aperture.

With a sharp dividing line between the filtered and non-filtered areas (such as a horizon over a water surface), small apertures are better since you do not want the sky colors to bleed into the water area.

In other cases, a large aperture may be preferred, producing a blurred outline that gradually changes and is less visible.

Filters for Infrared Photography

Filters are used in infrared photography to absorb blue and UV light so that only the deep red and the infrared rays reach the film. For black and white work, a deep red filter is recommended. For experimental and creative color work, any filter can be used. Yellow, red, green, blue, purple, and violet filters produce beautiful and unusual color effects with many subjects.

Exposure Increase

Most filters absorb light, so exposure must be increased. The amount of loss is mentioned in the instructions or may be engraved on the filter rim. The indication can be in f values or in filter factors. The two are not the same.

Filter Factors and f-stops/EV

Filter factor	1.5	2	2.5	4	6
Increase in exposure in f-stops or EV value	½	1	2½	2	2½

Filter factor	8	16	32	64
Increase in exposure in f-stops or EV value	3	4	5	6

Built-in exposure meters measure the light through the filter and compensate automatically, so you need not consider the filter factors. This may not apply to a polarizing filter. Ordinary, also called "linear polarizing filters," may not provide the correct meter reading with some built-in metering systems, depending on how the system works.

Filter manufacturers, therefore, introduced another type of filter, known as a circular polarizer. This type should give the correct meter reading with any built-in metering system and is usable with any camera, even those that also work with the ordinary linear type.

Quality of Filters

Filters used with high-quality lenses for critical photography must be made to the same quality standards. This is especially important when you use filters all the time, when you add filters to long focal length lenses, or when you combine filters. Glass filters are cleaned like lens surfaces: by blowing or brushing off dust or cleaning them with lens tissue (lens cleaner only if necessary). Never use lens cleaner or any other chemical solvent for cleaning plastic types. A soft brush or blower will remove dust. Grease or finger marks can be removed with a soft polishing cloth, if necessary, after you breathe on the filter surface. Avoid unnecessary brushing and cleaning. Place a lens cap over a filter on the lens, and store loose filters in a case.

Special Effect Filters

Special effect filters can change the colors, the sharpness, and the appearance of any scene. They can add stars and color fringes to the subject, or multiply a subject in any fashion. The choice of such filters is extensive. You can use them for fun. For serious, professional work you may want to be more careful.

"Avoid unnecessary brushing and cleaning."

The final image should not give the impression that the filter was used as a gimmick. The use of the filter must enhance the image. Some special effect filters create the opposite effect: the fog filter, for example, produces the effect of fog but does so evenly oven the entire image area. This is not the way we see fog. The foreground subjects closer to the camera are more distinctly visible than those farther away. Because the fog filter does not produce this result, its effect can look very artificial.

Working with UV Light

Photography in the UV range of the spectrum can be either UV or fluorescence photography. UV photography is limited to special types of applications, mainly in the forensic and medical fields.

Things that are invisible in regular light (retouching on paintings, alterations on checks and documents) become visible when photographed in UV radiation.

Regular lenses are usable for most UV work. When short range UV radiation is necessary, special lenses made from quartz rather than glass are necessary. Glass does not transmit those UV rays.

Since all films are sensitive to UV light, any film can be used for any type of work in this field. In most applications, black and white film shows everything you want to see. Color film, on the other hand, must be the choice for fluorescence work.

Fluorescence Photography

Fluorescence photography provides exciting possibilities for creating unusual images on color film. You can use daylight or tungsten film, each producing somewhat different colors. The subject that you photograph must be illuminated with UV light.

What you record on the film, however, is the light reflected from the subject: regular visible light. As a result, no special cameras, lenses or films are needed.

What you need are subjects that fluoresce. If the subject does not, you can paint it with fluorescent paint or lipstick. If the subject is illuminated with UV radiation, you can see the effect with your eyes so you know what works or does not and what it will look like on the film.

You need a light source that gives out UV radiation. Special fluorescent tubes marked BLB are available. They do not produce a great amount of light and are usable only for subjects that do not move, so you can use a fairly long shutter speed. More practical is electronic flash. All flash units, studio or portable, produce UV radiation. Since you only need the UV radiation, you want to eliminate most or all of the visible light. A Kodak 18A filter, placed over the flash unit, serves this purpose. Some manufacturers of studio lights also make special filters for this purpose.

A regular UV filter should be placed over the camera lens to absorb the UV rays which have a tendency to add a bluish cast to the image. Exposure is determined (as usual) with an incident meter, a reflected or built-in meter in combination with a gray card, or a flash meter if flash is used. I suggest that you make test exposures since different meters may react somewhat differently to UV light.

"...provides exciting possibilities for creating unusual images..."

CHAPTER TWELVE

Professional Soft Focus Photography

Creating a "soft touch" offers opportunities for producing beautiful images. The soft outlines add a glamorous touch to portraits, bridals, and fashion shots, at the same time reducing the need for negative or print retouching. A softness in images advertising beauty products or things associated with romance, food, or drinks can enhance the sales appeal. In landscapes, a soft touch can emphasize the shimmering highlights of a backlit scene.

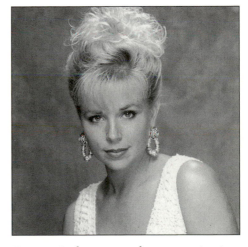

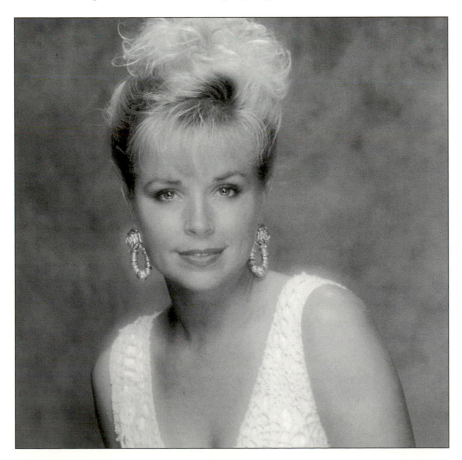

In most indoor or outdoor portraits, just a touch of softness is necessary (left) to make the image more romantic and reduce the harshness of a "straight" portrait produced with today's high quality lenses (above).

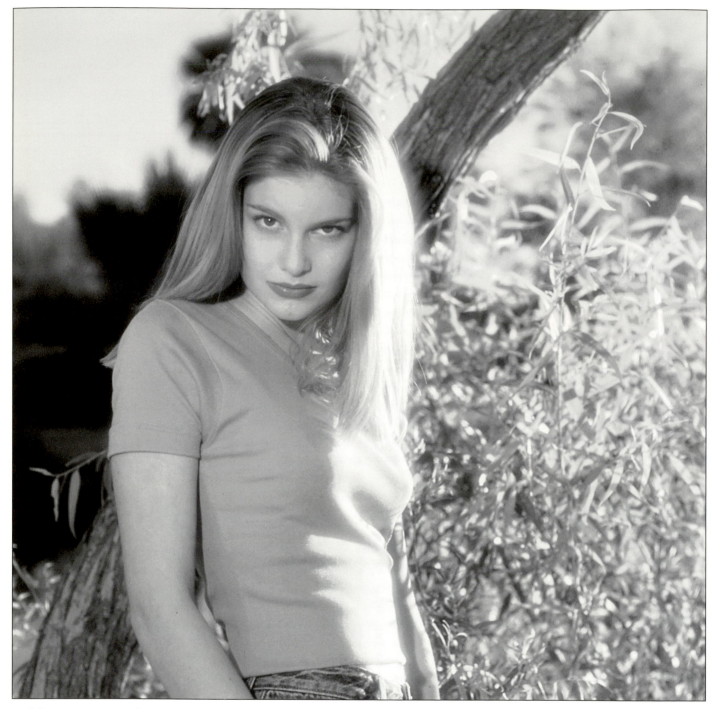

Soft focus images outdoors are most effective when the sunlight is used as a sidelight, as in this photo, or backlight.

Soft Focus Lens or Soft Focus Filter?

A "soft touch" can be produced on black and white or color film with soft focus lenses or with filters. But it is not necessary to invest in a special lens for producing a professional soft touch.

An effective professional soft touch can be created with soft filters added to the front of regular sharp lenses. You do not have to invest in another lens just for producing soft images and carry this additional lens on location. Filters offer other advantages over soft focus lenses. With a soft focus lens,

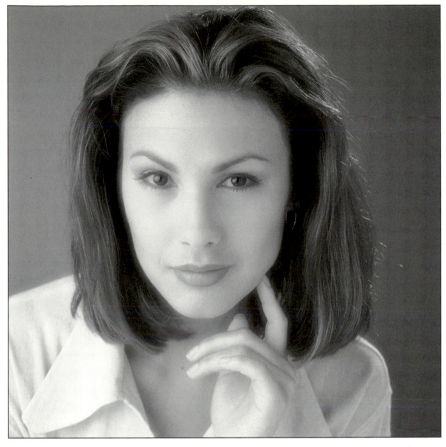

Good soft focus images need sharpness. Sharpness should be maintained even if heavier softness is applied. Note the sharpness in the hair and eyelashes.

all your soft pictures must be made at one focal length — the focal length of that special lens. With soft filters, you can select the focal length that is perfect for that particular shot, and you can switch from one to the other instantly. You can select a wide angle for an outdoor shot, the standard lens for a product shot, group picture or a full length portrait, and switch to the telephoto for the head and shoulder portrait.

With some soft focus lenses, the degree of softness changes with the aperture. But with most soft focus filters, the degree of softness is not affected by the aperture. I prefer this approach since I feel that a lens aperture is here to control depth of field, not the degree of softness. With filters, I can select the lens opening that produces the desired depth of field and I can change the aperture without changing the softness. Outdoor scenes, product shots, and close-ups may require the smallest aperture for depth of field. A portrait may call for a large aperture to blur the background.

With filters, you vary the degree of softness by changing the filter, not the lens aperture — and you can do so on all lenses.

When you evaluate the results produced by a soft focus lens or filter, examine the details in the picture under a good magnifying glass to determine whether the filter or lens produces an overall blur or maintains sharpness. This must be considered carefully because an effective soft focus image needs sharp contours with just a soft glow along the bright edges. It cannot have an overall appearance of unsharpness because this is not the way we see things. Our eyes are used to seeing sharp contours. There is a

"...you vary the degree of softness by changing the filter..."

difference between a professional soft touch and an unsharp image. If the filter maintains sharpness in the image, you have the additional benefit of focusing either with or without the filter on the lens.

The soft focus filter or lens should just "bleed" the highlights into the shaded areas, not create unsharpness.

Creating Effective Soft Focus Images

The desired degree of softness in an image may be determined by the subject and the lighting, or the use of the image. In most cases, however, the degree of softness is based on the personal preference of the photographer or the client. It is often difficult to make the decision when evaluating the subject on the focusing screen, especially on the smaller screen of 35mm cameras. I would suggest that you take the picture not only through one filter, but two or even three, unless you have used the filters before under similar conditions and know what the final results will look like.

For portraits, I prefer just a touch of softness and usually use the filter with the minimum effect. I have used stronger filters for some backlighted landscapes. Soft focus filters or lenses bleed the highlights into the shaded areas of the subject or background. This effect can be disturbing, especially when the "bleeding" goes into a background area, surrounding the subject with a halo. This happens mainly with dark backgrounds. Evaluate the image carefully on the focusing screen. Try to eliminate or reduce the "bleeding" by keeping the light away from bright subject areas, draping the model with darker clothing, or photographing the subject against a brighter background.

"...reduce the "bleeding" by keeping the light away from bright subject areas..."

Chapter Thirteen

Enhance the Image with Effective Composition

A good picture must have an attention-creating quality. This can be achieved by the subject itself, the lighting, the arrangement of lines, shapes and colors — all usually referred to as composition.

While a photograph should convey the personal view of the photographer, following guidelines for arranging the elements can help to create an image that is visually pleasing, powerful, and effective in the eyes of the average viewer.

Composing in the Square

Some photographers seem to feel that the arrangement of the elements in the square format is different from the rectangular shape. I do not feel that way. The same guidelines apply. You don't have to learn anything new when switching, for example, from the rectangular 35mm format to the 6x6cm square.

Subject Placement

A single subject in front of a background without any important picture elements usually belongs in the center in any format. That can apply to a frontal portrait, a product in an advertising image, or a close-up of a flower. A centrally placed single element creates an effective composition, but a somewhat static one. Usually a more moving image is created by placing the main subject approximately ⅓ from the left or right, or ⅓ from the top or bottom.

Balance

A subject placed to the side does not work with a plain background. Such an image lacks balance: a repetition of lines and shapes, or in color photography, a repetition of the color within the picture format. The "balance elements" must create less attention than the main subject, otherwise they become distracting. You usually do not want two equally attention-creating elements in a picture. Such an arrangement makes the eyes jump from one to the other.

"A good picture must have an attention-creating quality."

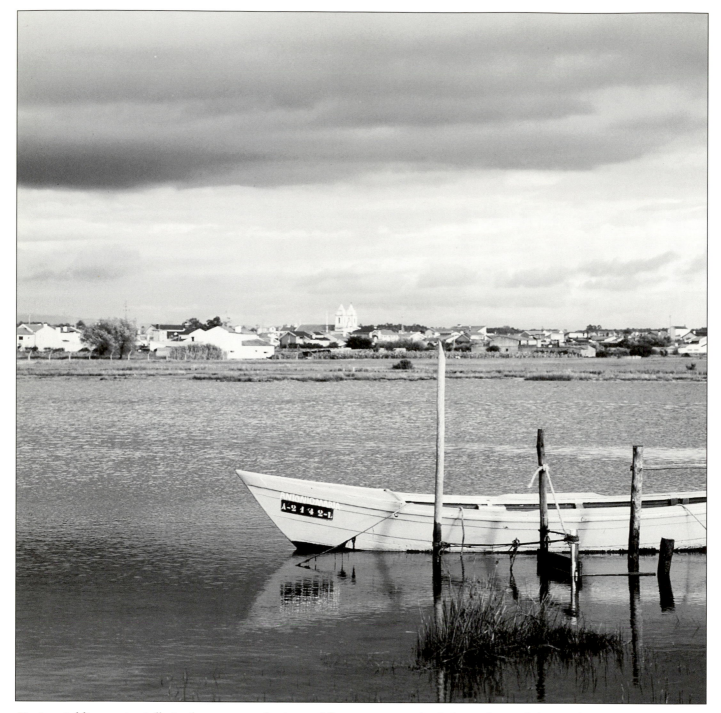

Horizontal lines, especially in the square or horizontal format, convey the feeling of peacefulness. This photo was taken in Portugal.

Lines

Horizontal lines create a feeling of peace and quiet in any format. Use or emphasize horizontals if that is the mood you want to create. For a more dynamic mood, emphasize verticals and diagonals. You can create diagonals artificially by taking some pictures with a tilted camera.

Pay attention to the placement of strong horizontal or vertical lines. Placing them in the center of the image can be effective when there is a

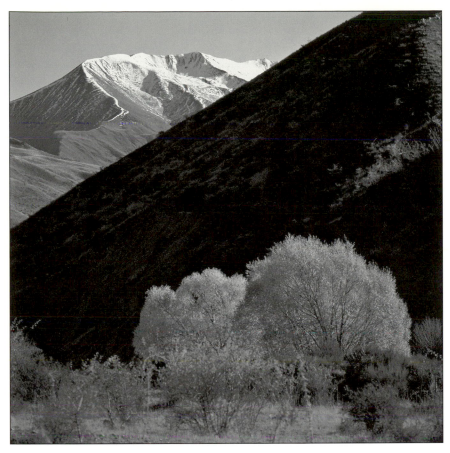

Vertical and especially diagonal lines make images in any format more dynamic. This photo was taken in New Zealand.

repetition of lines, shapes and colors on both sides, such as the subject on one side, its reflections on the other. Such a composition emphasizes the repetition but also splits the image into two equal halves which, in most cases, is not very effective. In most images in any format, strong verticals or horizontals (such as the horizon) are more effectively placed in the ⅓ position, about ⅓ from left or right, ⅓ from top or bottom. You now force the viewer to look at whatever you feel is more important: the sky if the horizon is ⅓ from the bottom, the landscape in the foreground if the sky covers only the top ⅓ of the image.

Attention-Creating Elements

In a photographic image, any element that is a different shape, size, or color or "moves" in a different direction creates attention. A red traffic light will attract attention if it is the only red in the picture. A small tree bent diagonally in the midst of large vertical trees will catch our eye because it "moves" in a different direction. So will the one boat that goes vertically among hundreds of boats going horizontally in a harbor scene. Use such "one and only elements" to attract a viewer's eye if they add to the picture, but avoid them if they might distract from what you are trying to show.

I find that many otherwise successful images are spoiled by distracting elements. Lines that are expected to be perfectly horizontal or vertical, (a horizon or the sides of a building) will distract if tilted even slightly. Bright

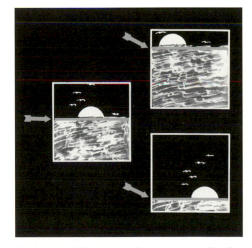

Dominant lines in the center split the image into 2 equal halves. A better placement, ⅓ to the top or bottom for example, can create a more dynamic picture.

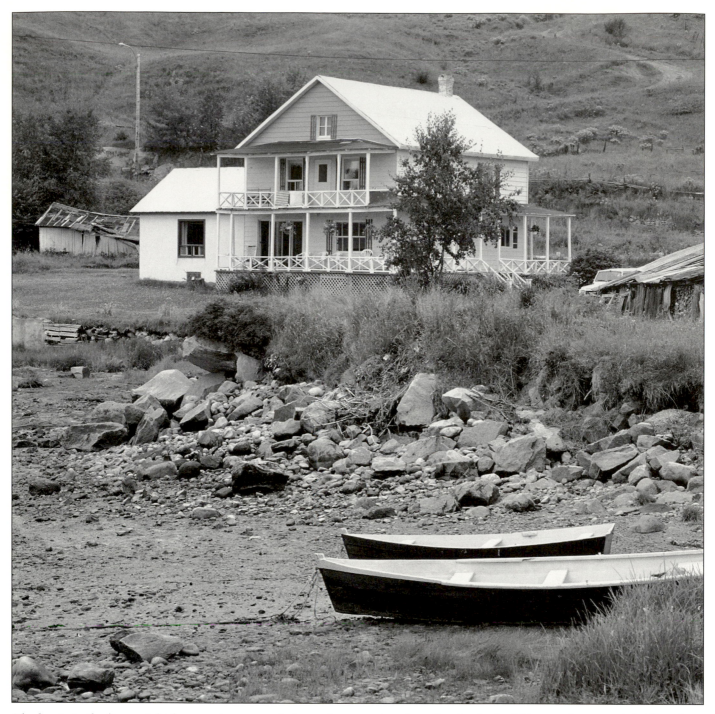

The boats in the lower right form an important balance by repeating the colors in the building on the upper left. This photo was taken in the Canadian Province of Quebec.

areas always attract attention, even if they are nothing more than highlights on a shiny surface. Such bright areas are especially distracting if they appear near the sides or corners of an image, leading the eye out of the picture.

Any subject partially cut off by the frame of the image and any dominant line cutting into the frame line of the image will catch a viewer's eye. As an example, our eye will instantly go to the church steeple that cuts into the picture frame below its top.

In principle, any attention-creating element is a plus in a picture if it leads the eye to the main subject, a negative if it makes the eye turn away from in.

Keep the Image Simple

Good images attract the eye and keep it in one place. They don't make the eye move all over the image, not knowing what is important or what the image is to convey, possibly even making the eye leave the image completely. Such an impression is frequently created by having too many elements within the picture frame. Simplifying by concentrating on one, or at least fewer, elements is frequently the best approach for creating more effective visuals.

After you take the first picture, always move in closer and look for other possibilities. In many cases, you will discover that the closer you go, the more you eliminate, and the more effective your visuals will be.

"Good images attract the eye and keep it in one place."

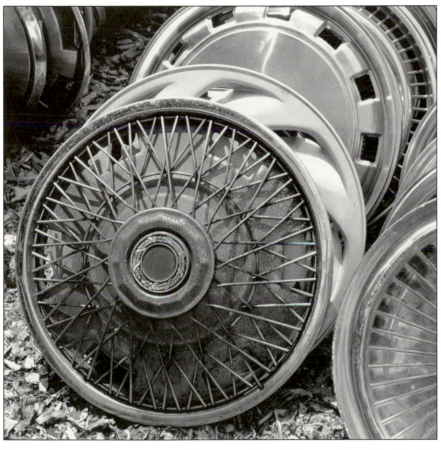

Remember, good images attract the eye and keep it in one place. Keeping the image simple creates some effective and visually powerful pictures.

CHAPTER FOURTEEN

Beyond the Picture Postcard

On your travels, you will undoubtedly be tempted to photograph the typical tourist sites: the monuments, buildings, and mountains that are all available on picture postcards. Nothing wrong with bringing home your own souvenirs, but your photographic appreciation and the enjoyment from those who see your pictures or slides will be highly rewarded if you go beyond the picture postcard.

With the worldwide communication that we have today, and with television in practically every home, the typical tourist sites are nothing new to most people. While enjoyable, most people prefer to see something new or at least see old things in a different way. There are many ways you can make your tourist pictures more rewarding to you and more interesting to your audience.

Try to photograph the well-known sites in a somewhat different way — perhaps from a different angle or from a different distance. It is probably not easy to find a better way. Professional postcard photographers have undoubtedly looked at the sites in many ways and have selected the most effective views for the tourist's souvenirs. I tried to find a way of photographing the Taj Mahal differently, but discovered that the most beautiful view is from exactly the same point as it is photographed by everyone else.

One solution is to photograph the statue, the building, *et cetera* as done on the tourist literature but follow up the postcard view with a few additional pictures from different angles or distances — add some close-up views of the details. This is an especially effective approach when shooting slides, resulting in a more moving slide presentation. You are actually using the movie approach of long, medium and close-up shots. Your zoom or tele lenses will come in handy.

Wide angle lenses can also help. They allow you to include foreground elements — a flower bed, a puddle of water, street signs — which may not appear in the picture postcard.

The easiest solution for creating a different image is offered by the light. Photograph the site in the early morning or late afternoon sunlight instead of the brilliant noon time sun usually found on the postcard picture. A strong sidelight with shaded and lighted areas may produce the desired difference. Create your images on an overcast, foggy, even rainy or snowy day. It gives

"Try to photograph the well-known sites in a somewhat different way…"

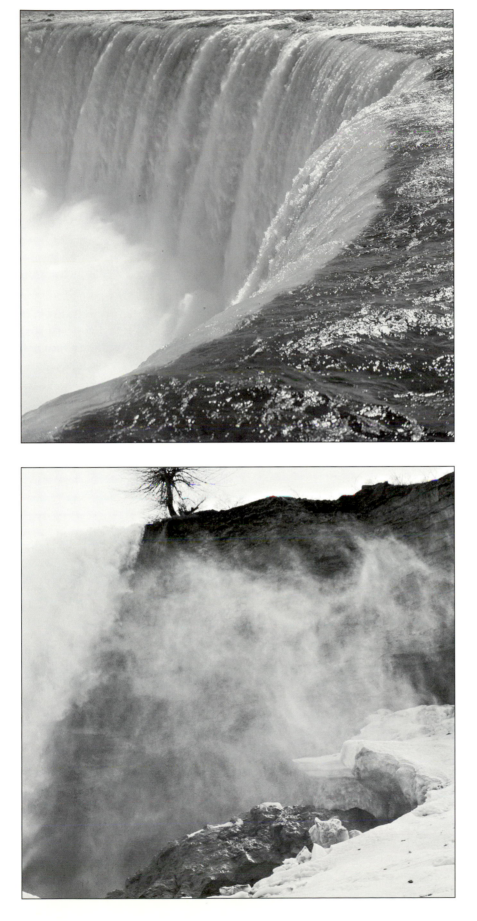

Two different views of Niagara Falls — the Canadian Falls in the summertime (top, left); and the American Falls in January (below).

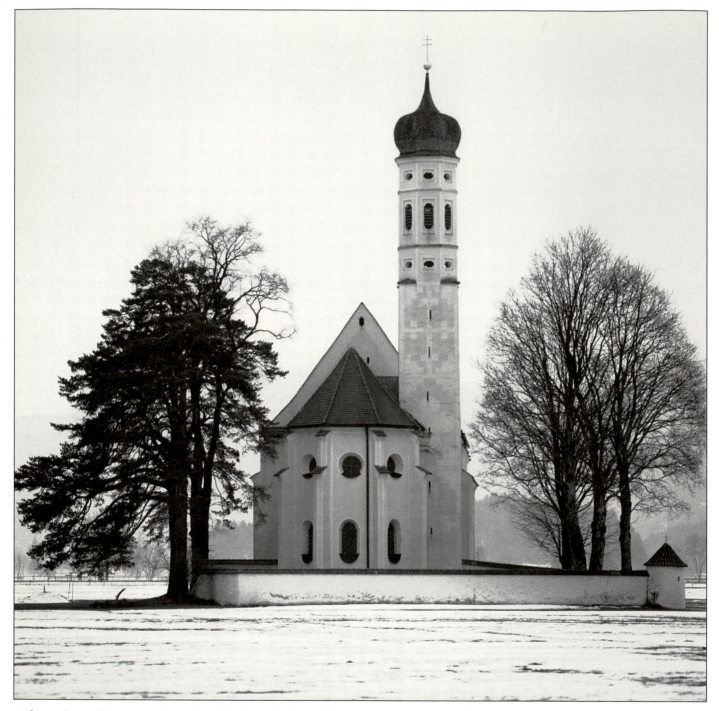

A foggy day adds a special mood and feeling. It also makes our travel pictures different from a typical picture postcard. This is especially helpful when photographing well-known tourist sites such as this church in Bavaria.

Opposite page: A built-in matrix or center metering system provides excellent exposures automatically for many outdoor subjects. This image was taken in Nova Scotia, Canada.

your images not only the "non-postcard view" but also a special mood. Photographing in a non-tourist season can also help. I find, for example, Niagara Falls more dramatic when covered with ice and snow.

A trip anywhere in the world will be more rewarding photographically if you don't limit your photography to the tourist sites. Try to come home with beautiful, perhaps unusual images of anything you see: the details in an iron gate, the colors on a boat, a line pattern in a field, a shadow pattern in a

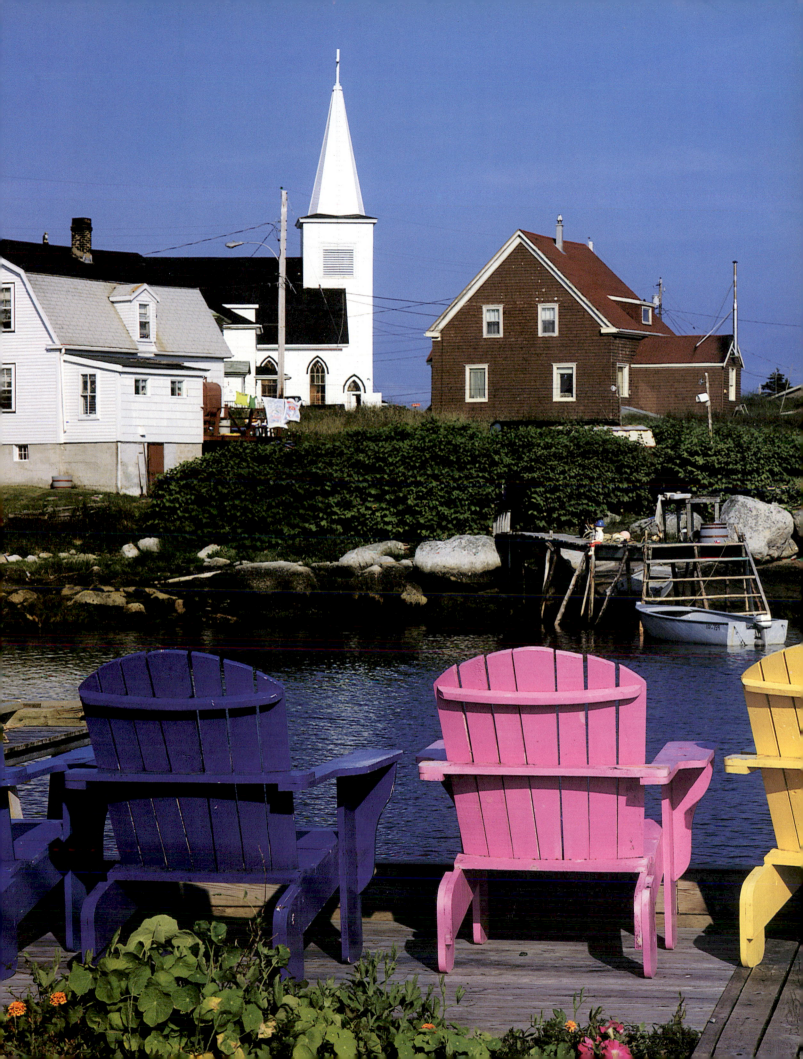

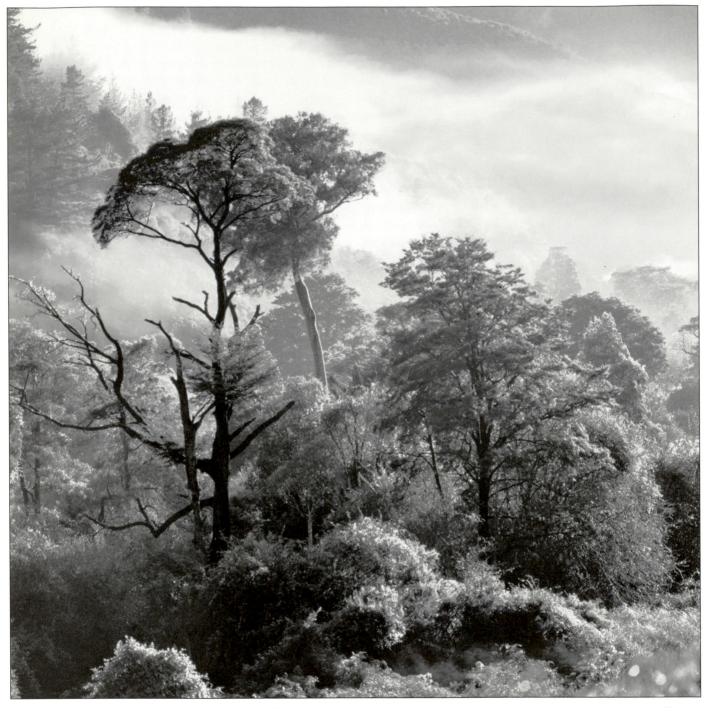

The early morning light can take on many different moods. Early morning fog in New Zealand adds a painterly effect to this photo.

street, the reflections on water or store windows. These details need not be typical of that area, they may be the same things that you find at home. As long as such images are composed with an effective arrangement of lines, shapes and colors, they will become a part of your personalized memories.

In many parts of the world, markets take place daily, or at least once or twice a week. They are great places to become more familiar with the area and the people, and great places to use roll after roll of film. As everywhere, don't limit yourself to overall shots. Go close. You find most wonderful arrangements of fruits, vegetables, handicrafts, jewelry, whatever they might sell. In most cases, photograph things as they are, where they are.

Don't forget the people. Marketplaces and flea markets are convenient places to get close to them. They are occupied and in many places do not object to being photographed. Should you ask permission? I follow the suggestion of a Mexican fellow photographer who took me to the marketplaces of the Indians who do not look favorably on being photographed. She said, "Just take the picture. If they don't like it, they will let you know and then you stop (or find out what it costs)." It worked in Mexico and in other places. However, since you probably want candid, not posed pictures, you will only succeed if you work fast.

Keep photography simple. A tripod is a burden and a nuisance. Leave it at home or in the hotel. Learn to hold your camera, even a medium format camera, steady. Practice before you go there.

Take advantage of all the automation you may have in your camera — automatic focusing and exposure — or learn how to focus and read the meter quickly.

You will be most successful when you catch the picture before the people realize that they are being photographed. This is the case not only in areas where people do not like to be photographed, but even where they are flattered when you photograph them — in Indonesia, for example. You will get a candid, natural picture rather than a posed one. You can always take a posed portrait after you catch the people candidly.

"Keep photography simple."

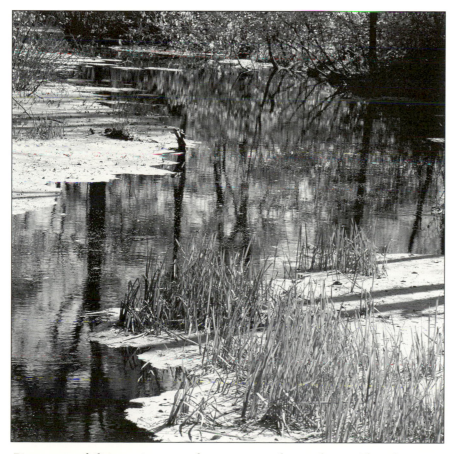

Picture possibilities exist everywhere — even close to home. This photo was taken in New Jersey.

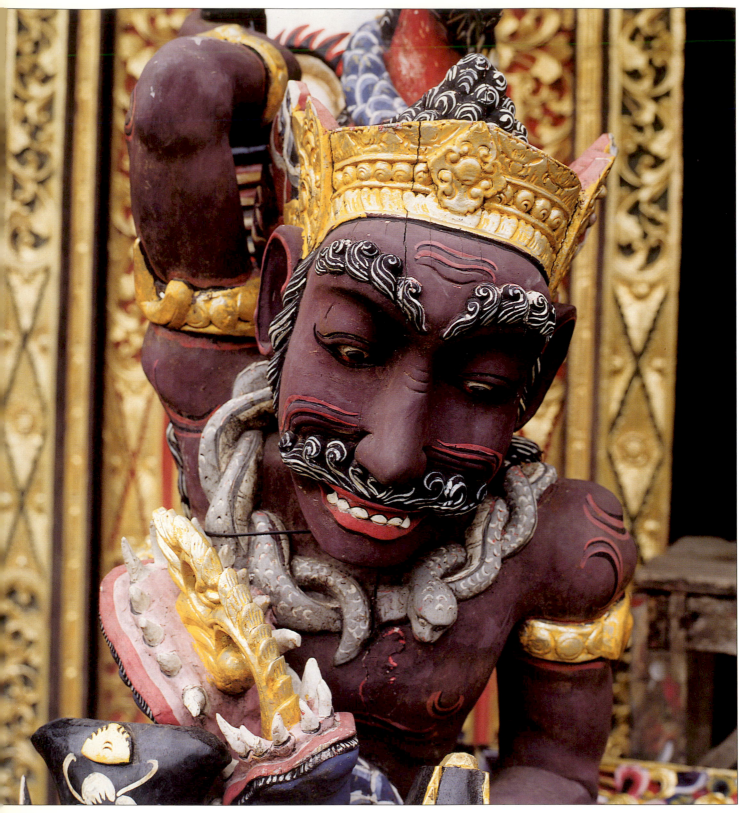

Close-up photo of a statue on sale in a Bali antique store shown on page 107.

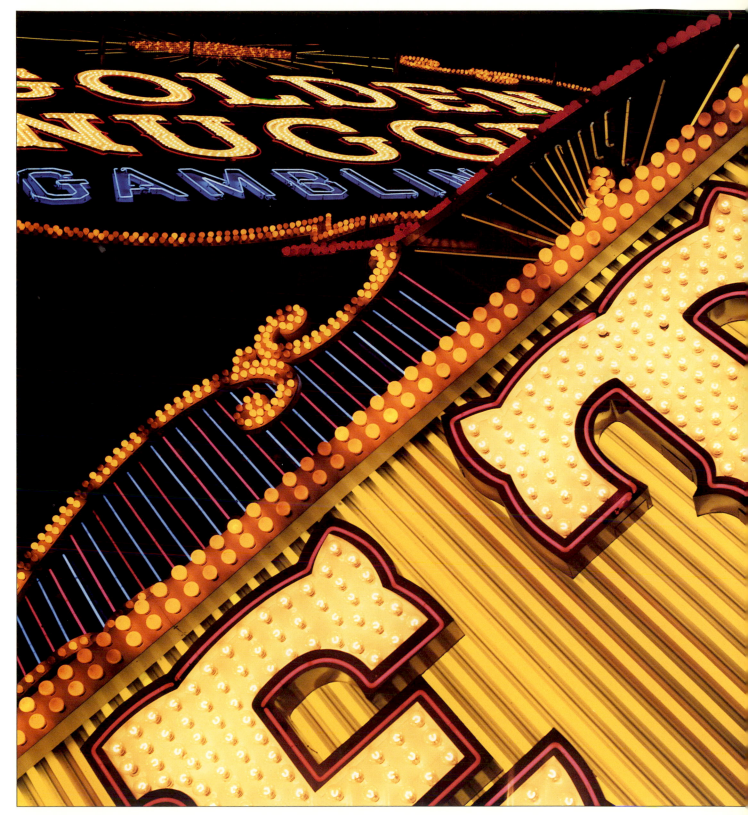

The dazzling lights of Las Vegas, from an unique angle, provide an excellent, yet different, example of a "picture postcard."

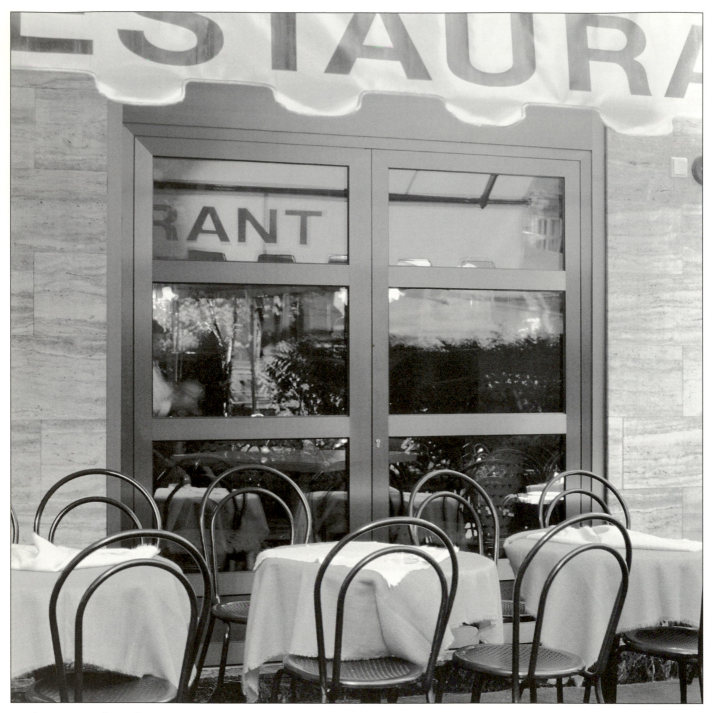

Ordinary everyday subjects can make interesting pictures too. This photo was taken in the early morning light in Vienna.

In most marketplaces, people are in shaded areas under umbrellas, even on sunny days. You may not need a faster film, but 400 ASA instead of 100 will allow you to use higher shutter speeds. This reduces the danger of camera or people motion. It also allows you to shoot at a smaller aperture so that small focusing errors still produce a good or at least acceptable image. With the proper fast shooting approach, longer focal length lenses are not necessary and, in my opinion, not even recommended. They present more problems with camera motion and need a longer distance,

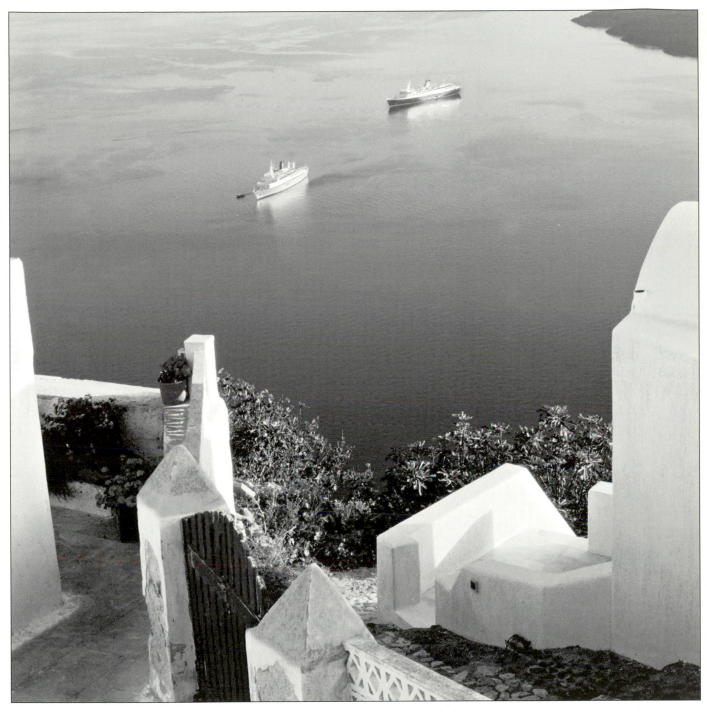

This image combines light and shade. It was taken in the late afternoon sunlight on Santorini in Greece.

which is frequently nonexistent in marketplaces. You want to be as close as practical. I have found lenses from 100 to 150mm to be ideal on my 6x6mm medium format camera. They are equivalent to focal lengths between 70 and 90mm on 35mm.

Flash is undoubtedly desirable in marketplaces but will make you more visible as a photographer. You may want to forget about it in places where you don't want to create attention and do your best with the existing light. If you do use flash, keep in mind that in an outdoor market, the existing

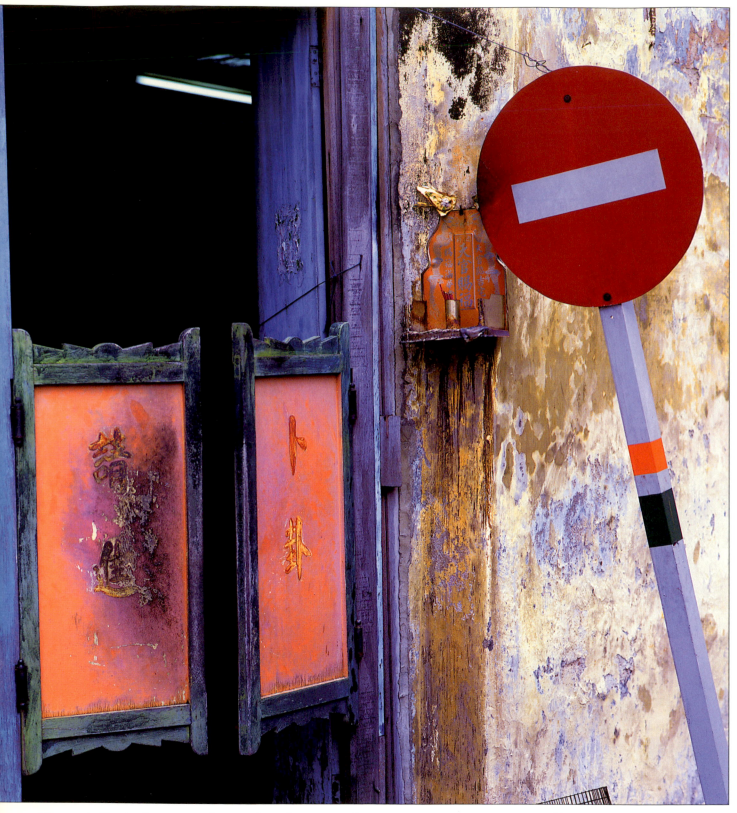

The most effective images are frequently nothing more than an interesting arrangement of lines, shapes, and colors. This photo was taken in Malaysia.

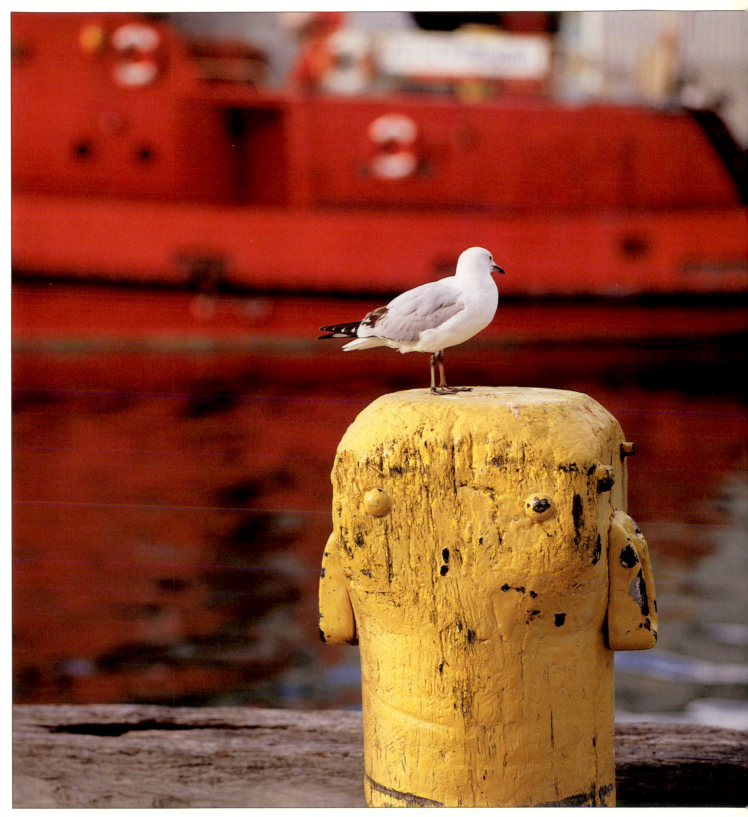

It was not the seagull that made me take this picture but the yellow colors on the post framed against the red colors in the background. This photo was taken in New Zealand.

daylight must remain the main light source. It should not be overpowered by the flash. The flash should just be used to lighten the shaded faces and eyes of the people.

You only need a little flash since you are close to people and probably working at relatively large apertures. Do not take a large professional unit. A small compact unit mounted on the camera or the flash built into your camera is sufficient. Reduce the flash illumination if possible by 1½ to 2 f-stops in relation to the daylight exposure. Set the flash fill function in a 35mm or

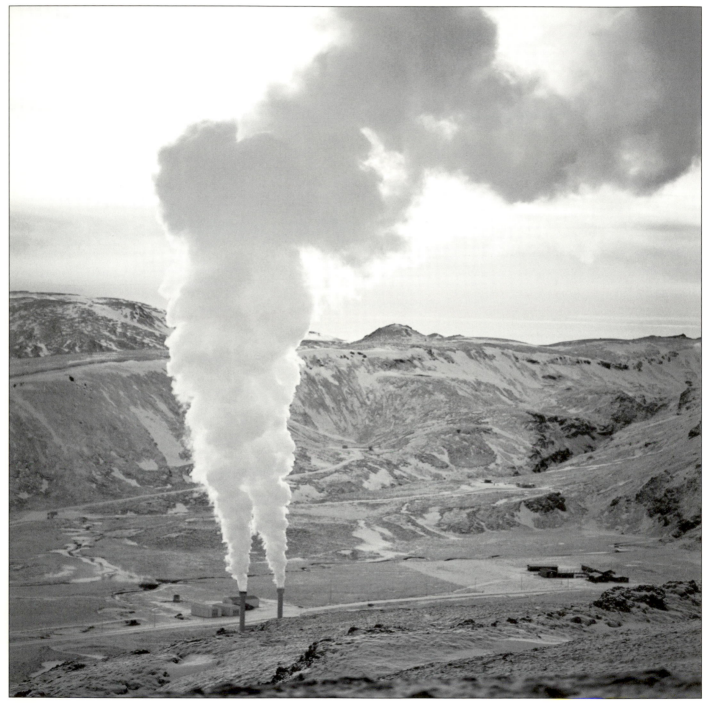

An unusual view that will make every photographer look for the camera even in the cold of a January day in Iceland.

medium format camera to minus 1½ to 2. On a dedicated system where the flash exposure is controlled by the ASA setting, set the ASA to 300 or 400 for 100 ASA film, to 1000 or 1200 for 400 ASA film.

In places where people like your presence and like to be photographed, you can become a real hero if you can "reward" people with an instant photograph. So if you work with a medium format camera with interchangeable film magazines, attach the Polaroid film back after you finish your photography and take one more picture to donate to your newly made friends.

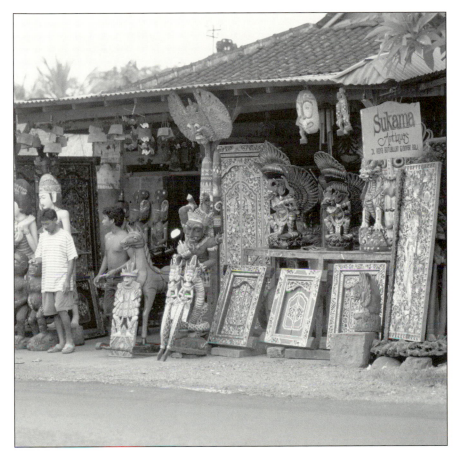

Here is a photo of an antique store in Bali.

The Pleasure of Photographing People

Photographing people anywhere in the world, but especially in other countries, can be your most rewarding experience. It brings you closer to the people. Even if you do not speak the language, there is usually some communication. Frequently, the people take an interest in what you are doing. They want to know where you come from and they may also be flattered that you take an interest in them. That is also the reason why I want to be close to the people using standard or short telephoto lenses, 110 to 150mm on my 6x6 medium format camera (70 to 100 on 35mm). I would never "hide" with long tele lenses for this work. It would take away all my enjoyment from people photography, and viewing such images would not bring back the memories of being with the people.

"Frequently, the people take an interest in what you are doing."

107

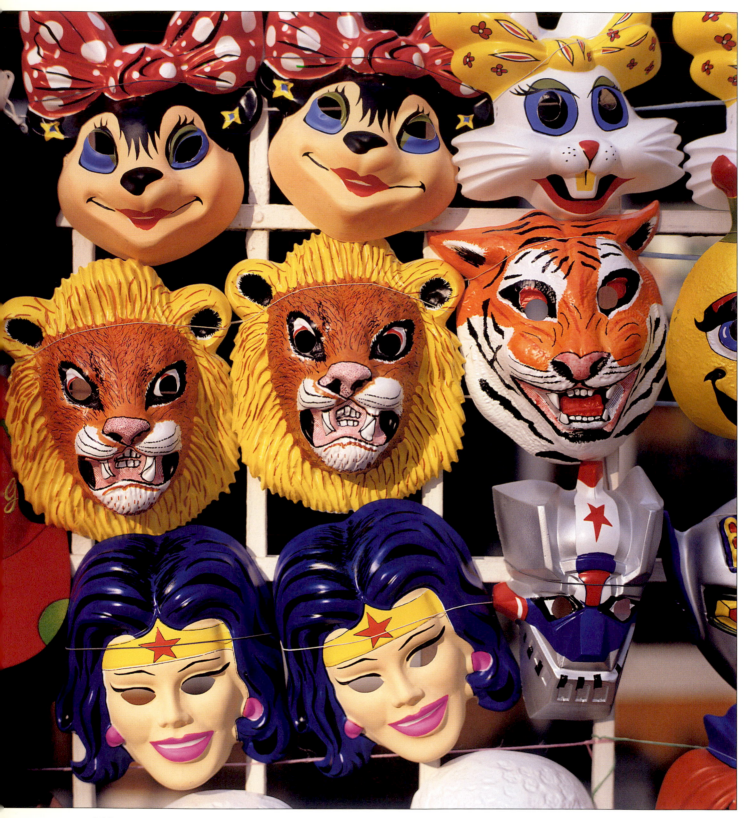

Items sold by street vendors can make wonderful pictures. These masks were on display on a street in Chile.

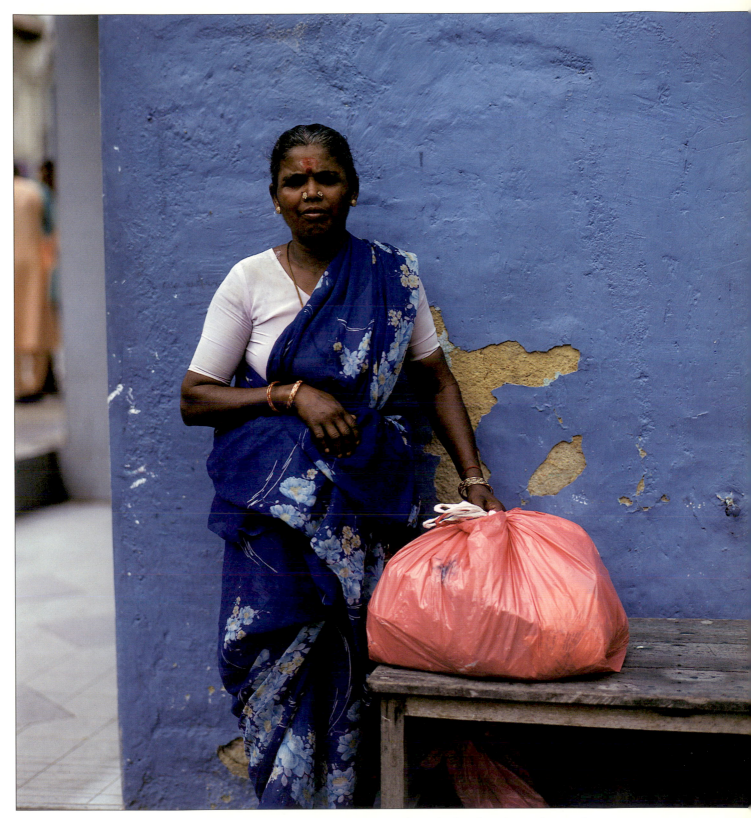

Here is a colorful example of photographing people outdoors. Notice how the bright colors enhance the image.

CHAPTER FIFTEEN

Photographing People Outdoors

I don't want to call this chapter "Outdoor Portraiture" as this term is commonly associated with and limited to the typical professional portrait approach for photographing groups or individuals with the final image framed and displayed in a dominant place in the home or office. Being part of the home or office decor, you want something that looks a little more like a painting.

This "painting" feeling can be emphasized by the finishing of the print and the framing. Finishing the print often includes darkening the corners, which unfortunately, in many portraits, is done so excessively that it looks unnatural and objectionable.

What I want to discuss here is not the "fireplace portrait" approach but just some better ways to take pictures of people we normally photograph — our family, friends, neighbors, or perhaps strangers that we use as non-professional models.

There are many simple ways to get away from the typical snapshot approach and to record people, especially young people, in a natural way but also in a way where they look more like professional models. Your pictures can look more like illustrations from fashion magazines. As an additional benefit, I feel these ideas will make your photography more enjoyable and the images will give your "models" great enjoyment, especially 20, 30 or 40 years from now.

To photograph people well, we must get away from the approach of just photographing whoever stands in front of the camera and in whichever way they stand there. Pay attention to the light, the background, the surrounding area, and help people with the pose.

Lighting

The choice of lighting is limited if the picture must be made outdoors at a specific location at a specific time. If the choice of time and location are open, your chances for success are unlimited.

Sunlight shining into people's faces must be avoided. Such light is flat, harsh and people have problems keeping their eyes open. Sunlight, on the other hand, can be beautiful as a backlight or a sidelight. I recommend it

"Pay attention to the light, the background, the surrounding area..."

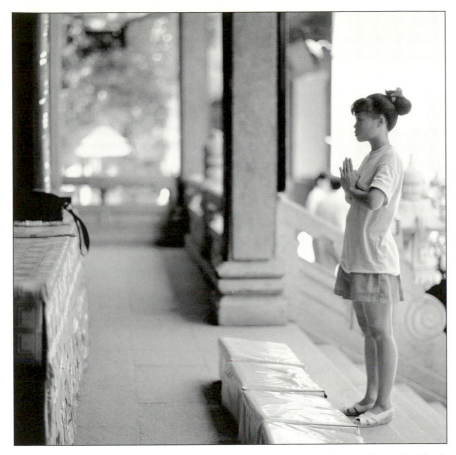

A people picture made effective by the composition — placing the girl's black hair against the bright background which immediately attracts the eye and keeps it there.

especially for photographing young people. Sunlight adds a feeling of life and happiness and is therefore often used in fashion photographs. To reduce the contrast between the lighted and shaded areas, you must add light to the shaded areas. This can be done with reflectors or flash. Flash is not only the simplest and most practical approach, but also allows the model to move without worrying too much about the light. With reflectors, every change in the pose may require an adjustment on the reflector. Such a picture is more likely to become a static portrait. You want people, especially young ones, to be able to move, be alive, and enjoy themselves being photographed.

Flash is my suggestion for a fill light. Since people pictures are usually done at larger apertures to blur the background, you do not need much fill light. So don't necessarily carry a big flash unit. A small flash unit, right on top or built into the camera serves the purpose well. The flash must appear just as fill light, hardly recognizable. This is to be a daylight picture, not a flash picture. Reduce the flash the equivalent of at least one f-stop, two may be better for producing a natural looking daylight picture.

Since the flash is rather weak, I have never found a problem with red eye effect, even if the flash is right on the camera. I suggest, however, enlarging the flash head surface with a little soft box, if practical, as suggested in the flash chapter. Such a box softens the flash light, making the use of flash even less noticeable. The flash now looks like a natural fill-in light.

"Sunlight adds a feeling of life and happiness..."

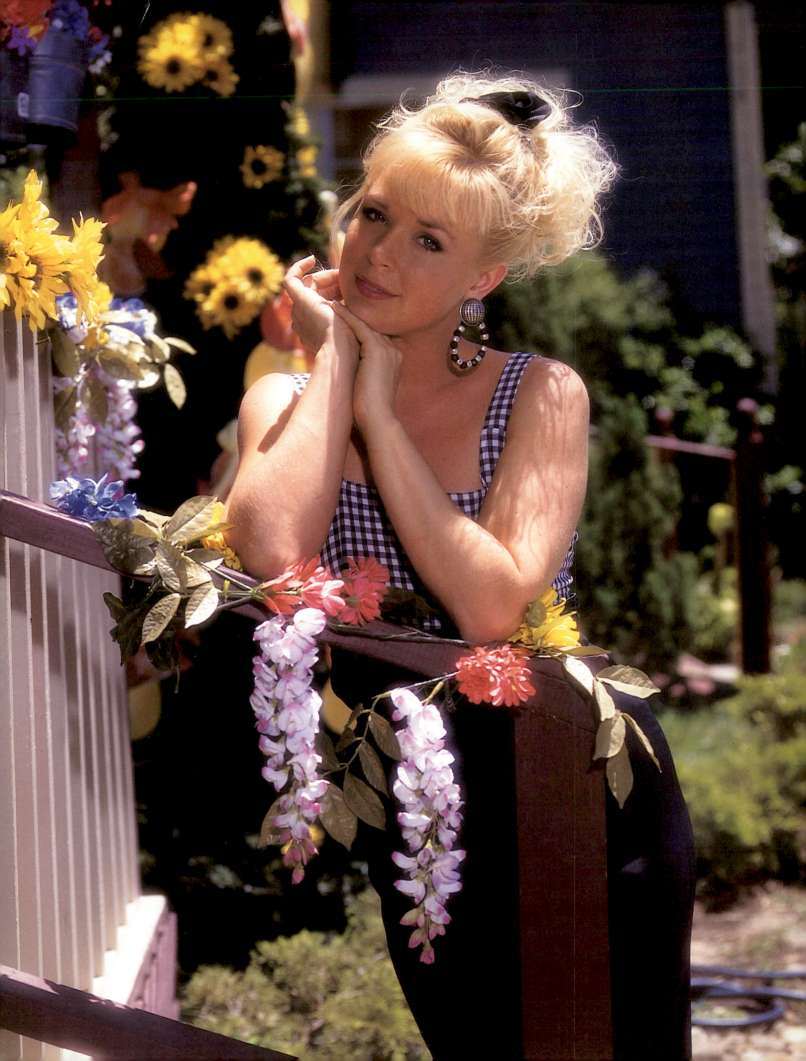

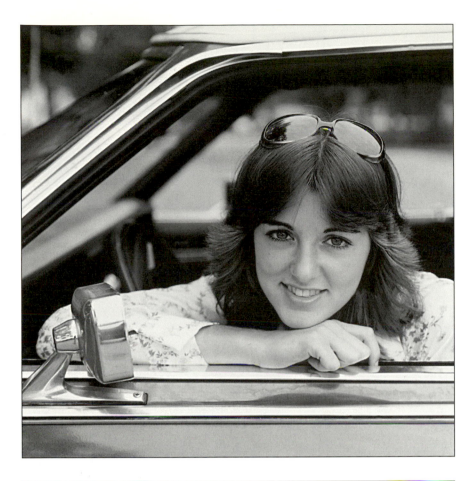

An open car window makes it easy for anyone to fall into a natural pose. The eyeglasses, as a prop, add another nice touch (left). Asking your "model" to walk on a railroad track can hardly fail to result in a delightful, natural pose with lively expressions (below).

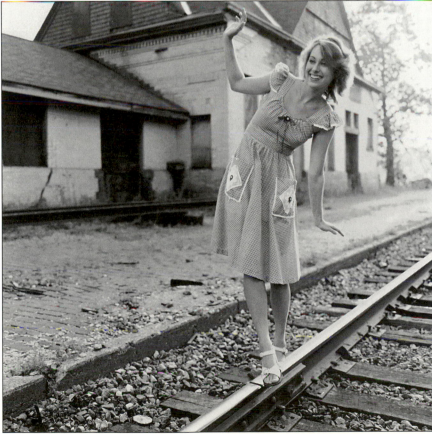

Opposite page: Another bright and colorful example illustrating the wonderful possibilities of photographing people outdoors. Fill flash and a Softar soft focus filter were used.

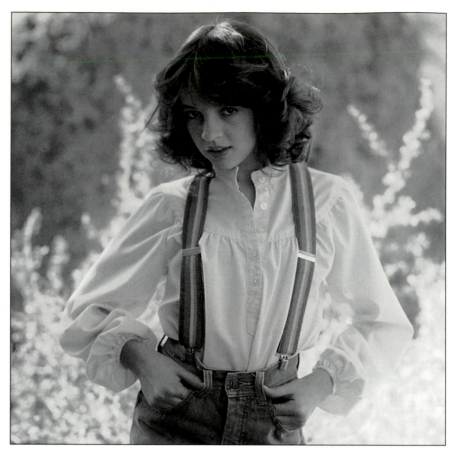

Pay attention to the placement of arms and hands. Pockets and belts can provide helpful ideas and make useful props.

Pay careful attention to the sunlight. Used as hairlight, the light is usually more effective if it comes slightly from the side instead of from straight back. This corresponds to what a portrait photographer does in the studio. Avoid the sunlight hitting the tip of the nose. Such a highlight creates too much attention.

For the professional portrait photographer, the soft light of an overcast day or the diffused light in a shaded area is frequently preferred. Whether it produces a better picture is questionable, but the effect is more subdued but not necessarily flat.

Even on an overcast day or in complete shade, there is always more light coming from one side — you can see this clearly when watching the light on the model's face or body. Ask the person to turn the face or body in either direction and the subtle differences become more obvious.

Your images will be better when you photograph into the light, in the direction where the existing light produces lighter and darker areas on the face and body.

This approach is especially effective in black and white work. With color film, flash can help even in the diffused light of an overcast day or shaded area. The flash may do no more than add a little light into the eyes, but it will also help to produce better colors under the unknown color qualities of the light. Adding flash will definitely result in better flesh tones.

A beautiful light (usually not requiring flash) exists on a foggy day. You end up with a beautiful portrait almost regardless of where or how you

"Avoid the sunlight hitting the tip of the nose."

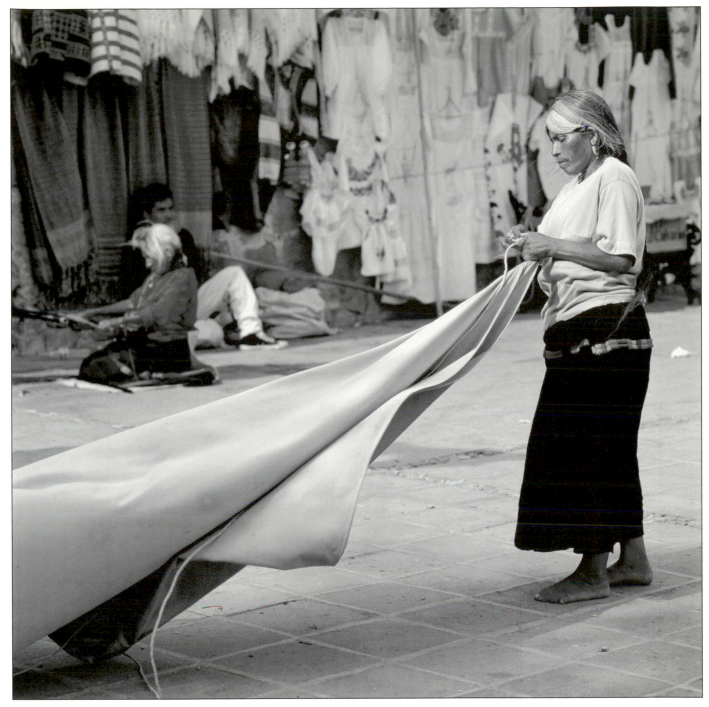

People pictures can be successful in the candid fashion, with the people unaware of being photographed. This photo was taken in Mexico.

take the picture. Also, don't forget the early morning or late afternoon light. It can be softer, certainly more beautiful, than the light produced by the midday sun.

The warmer light, however, produces warmer flesh tones. This is not necessarily objectionable and can even be beautiful if the entire image conveys the early morning or late afternoon feeling. That means including a rather large background area that conveys this mood. It usually works in a three quarter or full length portrait, not in a head and shoulder portrait.

"The background is an important part of an outdoor portrait..."

Location & Background

A main reason for photographing people outdoors is the variety of locations and settings that exist everywhere. The background is an important part of an outdoor portrait: it is the part of the image that can make it different from a portrait done in the studio. That is the reason why I personally like the square format for this purpose. The additional space on the side allows me to include more of the background area without making the person smaller. While this does not apply so much for a headshot, it certainly does for three quarter and full length pictures. Including a larger background area is also the reason why many professional portrait photographers like to use wide angle, or even fisheye lenses for this purpose.

Select a location that enhances the image and is appropriate for the outfit the person is wearing. A country location (fields, forests) is fine for casual wear. For more formal wear, you may want to consider a town setting that includes beautiful or interesting architecture.

Colors must enhance rather than distract from the image. A colorful background is great when the person is wearing white or black. For more colorful outfits, subdued colors in the background are more appropriate. Backgrounds somewhat out of focus or completely blurred are obviously less distracting. Use a larger aperture and/or a longer focal length lens.

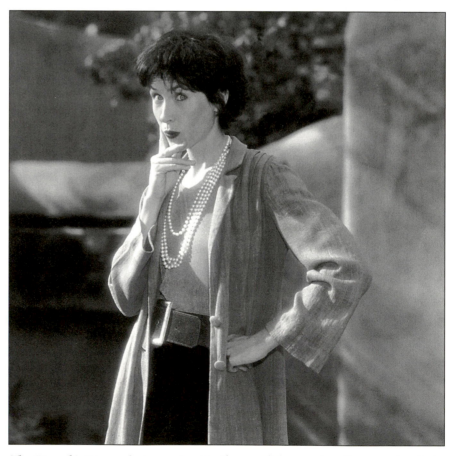

The "posed" approach, in contrast to the candid one, gives the opportunity to pay more attention to the light and background.

Longer lenses also include a smaller background area and will make it easier to eliminate distracting background elements: billboards, cars, or people, for example. With longer lenses, a slight change in camera angle can change the background drastically.

The Professional Touch

Most fashion photographers will tell you that it is the styling, the clothes, the hair style, and the make-up that make an "ordinary" person look like a professional model. While we probably will not use professional help for that purpose, volunteers who know something about clothes, can apply good make-up, and know how to style hair can always be found. Since most young women like to look like the professionals in the fashion magazines, ask your model to wear something that is not completely ordinary, something that flatters and enhances her character.

Once the "model" is in front of the camera, little suggestions from you can go a long way in making your model look like a pro. The best place to start is with the legs. Ask the model to place the weight on one leg. This allows the model to place the other leg almost anywhere: to the side, in front, crossed over the other leg, *et cetera*. It almost invariably will result in a more graceful pose. Rather than just telling the model what to do, actually demonstrate it. Place your legs where you would like to see them. Next, suggest turning the body to one side and the other, perhaps combined with a slight tilt which may result in a more graceful curved line. I usually worry last about the head, again asking the model to turn the head to one side and the other, watching both the pose and the lighting.

Placement of arms and hands seems to be a major problem for many people. Whatever is done should be natural: they should be placed somewhere where the model might normally keep them — pockets, underneath a belt, on the cheek or chin, even in the hair or just floating out in the air. Almost anything looks better than having arms and hands just hanging down.

While trying out these ideas, make it clear to the model that you are just experimenting, not shooting, and that you will tell them when you are ready to take the picture. It is tiring for anyone to stand in front of a camera, watched constantly. Make it easy for them, make sure they enjoy working with you. Their appreciation for your concern will be visible in the pictures.

Where do you get ideas for photographing young people? Look through the fashion magazines. There are always new ideas and trends in this competitive field. While many of the ideas are not usable for our approach, you will find many ideas regarding location, lighting, posing, placement of arms and hands, that you can duplicate. You can also use these illustrations to convey to your model what you are trying to accomplish.

These are some suggestions for producing better personalized portraits in your hometown or during your travels, while at the same time enjoying what you are doing. Keep in mind: good lighting is the most important key to success.

"...little suggestions from you can go a long way in making your model look like a pro."

117

Glossary

Advanced photo system: A relatively new film format, smaller than 35mm, that offers mainly advantages in film loading, printing and storing of images. The images can be recorded in three different formats: standard, wide and panoramic. The smaller format also allows producing more compact cameras.

Aperture: The size of the opening of the lens diaphragm. The maximum aperture of a lens is obtained by dividing the focal length of the lens into its entrance pupil (known to the lens designer).

Apochromatic lens: When designing photographic lenses, the designer is mainly concerned about correcting the chromatic (color) abberation for two colors, usually red and blue. Such a design can result in a high quality lens without noticeable color fringes in all but the longest focal lengths. Such lenses are known as achromatic. Eliminating color fringes completely, and producing the best edge sharpness in long focal length lenses, may require a lens that is corrected for three colors, usually red, blue and green. Such a lens is apochromatic. There is also a type known as Super Achromat which is corrected for more than three colors.

Aspheric lens: A lens element with one or two aspheric surfaces. Such elements are used in some photographic lenses. Since aspheric lens elements are difficult to manufacture, lens designers will not employ them unless absolutely essential. They will always try to obtain the required lens quality with the use of spheric lens elements.

Average brightness: In photography, a subject that reflects 18% of the light is considered average brightness (gray card). Reflected light meters are adjusted to provide the correct lens settings for a subject of average brightness.

Bellows: A flexible connection between the camera and lens. It is usually an accessory for 35mm and medium format cameras where it allows moving the lens further from the film plane for close-up photography. A bellows is also a part of most large cameras and some medium format types where it is used for focusing or for shift and tilt control.

Blurred motion: An unsharpness on the film that is caused by either the subject or the camera moving while the shutter is open to produce the image. While unacceptable in most images where the highest quality is required, the blur can also be used effectively to convey the feeling of motion, (sports or water for example). The slower the shutter speed the more enhanced the effect.

Cable release: An accessory that can be attached to the camera to release the camera without touching the release button. Recommended when working at longer shutter speeds to reduce the danger of camera movement. Some cable releases have a lock, helpful for very long exposures. A cable release is not needed for hand-held photography.

Close-up photography: Refers to photographing small subjects from close distances. There is no standard setting dividing the line between close-up and long distance photography. The dividing line is frequently based on the minimum focusing distance of the lens and where the need for the use of close-up accessories starts. With macro lenses, a good range of close-up photography can be done without the need for accessories.

Composition: Means making an effective, pleasing arrangement of lines, shapes and colors within the picture format.

Dedicated flash: A camera/flash system where the flash unit is electronically dedicated to the camera, measuring the flash through the camera lens. A sensor in the camera measures the flash (usually reflected off the film plane) and turns the flash off when the proper amount for correct exposure is reached.

Depth of field: The range of sharpness in front and behind the focused distance that is considered acceptably sharp in the final image. Depth of field is increased by closing the lens aperture. Depth of field is a calculated figure and not dependent on the lens design.

Digital camera: A camera where the image is recorded and stored electronically, not on film. Some medium format cameras can be used for digital recording by attaching a digital camera back instead of a rollfilm magazine.

Diopter: In principle, diopter is used to indicate the focal length of a lens, especially in eyeglasses. One diopter is equal to a 1 meter focal length. In photography, diopter is used in connection with close-up lenses and viewfinder eyepieces, in relation to correcting the camera viewfinder eyepiece to the photographer's eyesight.

Double exposure: When two or more images are recorded on the same piece of film, usually for creating a special effect.

Electronic flash: An excellent, bright source of light that can be used alone or in combination with daylight as both have the same color temperature. A large amount of light can be produced by a small and lightweight unit that can be mounted on the camera. Many cameras have a built-in flash.

Electronic imaging: A technology that allows producing black and white or color images electronically, eliminating the need for film, film processing and the use of chemicals.

Exposure meter: A device that measures the light or the subject brightness and gives us the aperture and shutter speed figures. The meter can be built into the camera or can be a separate accessory.

Fill light: Light used in addition to the main light to add illumination to dark or shaded areas. Electronic flash or reflectors are usually used for this purpose.

Film plane: The position of the film in the camera body or film magazine. Focusing distances are always measured from the film plane.

Film reflectance: The amount of light that is reflected off the film surface. May have to be considered in a dedicated flash system where the sensor measures the light reflected off the film plane.

Film sensitivity: Indicates how sensitive the film is to light, and determines the aperture and/or shutter speeds that are necessary to record a properly exposed image on the film. A film with a higher ISO number is more sensitive and therefore recommended in low light levels.

Filter factor: A figure indicating how much light a filter absorbs, thus requiring an increase in exposure when the filter is used. Filter factors are not, however, equivalent to f-stops.

Fisheye lens: A lens that is designed so the angle of view diagonally is much greater (usually 180 degrees) in relation to the angle of view horizontally or vertically. They produce an image with curved lines outside the center area.

Fixed focus: A lens found in point and shoot cameras that cannot be adjusted for different subject distances. The focal length is usually short and the aperture relatively small so that the depth of field covers a satisfactory distance range with acceptable sharpness.

Floating lens element: A wide angle lens design where some of the lens elements can be moved. Used in retrofocus wide angle designs to improve the image quality at close distances.

Focal length: The distance from the principal plane in the lens (known to the lens designer) to the point at which the lens forms an image of a subject at infinity. The focal length is always engraved on the lens. The focal length of a lens is the same regardless where and how it is used or regardless what film format it is to cover.

Focusing hood: A foldable viewfinder that is standard on most medium format cameras. It is usually interchangeable with a prism viewfinder.

Focusing range: The minimum and maximum distances at which sharp images can be produced without the use of any accessories.

Focusing screen: In single lens reflex and large format cameras, the image is viewed on a focusing screen rather than an optical viewfinder. On large format and special medium format cameras, the focusing screen is added to the camera in place of the film holder or magazine. On single lens reflex cameras, the mirror projects the image to the focusing screen before the image is made. Focusing screens come in many different versions, also with the addition of micro-prisms, split image rangefinders, checked lines *et cetera*.

Full frame fisheye lens: An image produced in a full frame fisheye lens covers the entire film area. Other fisheye lenses just produce a circular image in the center of the film. Full frame fisheye types have much wider applications.

High resolution film: A film with a high resolution and fine grain that is therefore capable of producing the utmost image sharpness. Films with lower sensitivities usually have these characteristics.

Hyperfocal distance: The distance setting on a lens that provides depth of field to infinity.

Image distortion: Refers to anything in the image that does not appear the way it looked to our eyes. Most image distortions are not created by the lens or camera but by the way the camera or lens was used. Image distortions can also be created artificially while the image is made or afterwards.

Image perspective: The size relationship between subjects at different distances as recorded in the camera. Perspective in a photograph is determined by the camera position, the distance between the lens and the closest subject.

Image sharpness: A visual perception of the amount of detail that is recorded or recognized on the film or the final image. The sharpness of a photographic image is however not so much determined by the amount of detail that is visible but the edge sharpness within the subject details.

Incident meter: An exposure meter that measures the light that falls on the subject that we are photographing. The reading is unaffected by the brightness or color of the subject.

Interchangeable film magazines: In medium format cameras, the film may be loaded into a separate, removable film magazine. This allows changing from one type of film to another in the middle of the roll of film.

Internegative: A color print from an original color transparency is usually produced by making first a color negative from the transparency. This negative is called an internegative. The color print is then made from this negative.

ISO: An international standard to indicate the sensitivity of a film. A higher number means a film with a higher sensitivity, a faster film.

Large format: Refers to image sizes larger than the medium format, usually 4x5 or 8x10 inches recorded on sheet film.

Lens elements: A single lens within the camera lens. These lens elements may be single components in the lens or they may be cemented together with one or two other lens elements to form a lens component.

Lens plane: The position of the lens in relation to the film plane. The two must normally be parallel to each other. On large format and some medium format cameras, one can be shifted or tilted in relation to the other to increase the range of sharpness or eliminate the need for tilting the camera.

Lens shade: A lens shade can be an accessory or it can be part of the lens. It eliminates unwanted light from reaching the lens and causing flare. A lens shade must be used even with multi-coated lenses as the two serve different purposes. The lens shade reduces flare by eliminating the unwanted light, the multi-coating does the same but with the light needed to form the image on the film.

Loupe: A magnifying glass that is used to check the sharpness and quality of a negative or transparency. Such a loupe may show the entire negative area but in such a case is undoubtedly of a lower magnification. For examining image sharpness, a loupe with a higher magnification (8x or 10x) is preferable even if it does not cover the entire negative area.

Low dispersion glass: The various lens elements within a photographic lens are made from different types of glass with the main difference being the refractive index of the glass. The refractive index refers to the angle at which the light is bent when it enters and leaves the glass. Low dispersion glass has an uncommon refractive index that may be helpful or necessary in designing certain lens types.

Macro lens: Usually a lens where the focusing control can be set to much closer distances than on an "ordinary" lens. Such a lens may eliminate the need for close-up accessories. The term "macro" may also refer simply to the fact that such a lens is designed optically to produce the best image quality at close distances.

Medium format: A film format larger than 35mm but not as large as 4x5 inches. It is a film format that should combine some of the benefits and advantages of each. The most popular medium formats are 4.5x6cm, 6x6cm, 6x7cm and 6x8cm. Medium format images are usually recorded on 120 or 220 rollfilm.

Mirror lock up: A feature found in some SLR cameras. Allows moving the mirror manually from the viewing to the taking position before the image is made. This reduces the danger of the mirror motion producing unsharpness on the film.

Monopod: A single support post for the camera which at shorter shutter speeds can serve the same purpose as a tripod. A monopod is more convenient for carrying and faster in use. A monopod can be equipped with the same heads used on tripods.

Motordriven film advance: A camera where the film is advanced to the next picture by means of a motordrive. The motor can be built into the camera or can be an accessory motor winder that can be attached to the camera. Motordriven film advance may allow faster shooting. Being able to keep the eye in the viewfinder of the camera however is the major benefit of a motor winder in most photography.

MTF diagrams: The best and generally used method to show the sharpness of a lens. With the Modulation Transfer Factor usually on a vertical axis, the curves of different spatial frequences indicate the image quality over the entire image area. The idea is based on the fact that image sharpness as seen by our eyes is not so much based on the amount of detail we see (resolution) but on the edge sharpness. Some manufacturers publish these curves based on what the computer says the lens should produce, others are based on the performance of the actual lens as made and sold. The latter is the only type that is meaningful.

Multi coating: Used on all high quality lenses today. The coating reduces the amount of light reflected on the glass surface and thus reduces flare and increases the contrast and color saturation.

Panoramic format: An image format that is at least twice as long in one dimension as in the other. Such images can be produced in APS and special panoramic medium format cameras. Panoramic images can be produced in some other cameras with masks or special magazines. The final image can also be changed into a panoramic by cropping.

PC card: A removable card that stores a larger number of data (pictures) in a digital camera. The image on the card can be viewed on a computer or TV screen or can be made into a print. In a way, the card is what a roll of film is in a film camera.

Perspective control: A feature built into special lenses, teleconverters or cameras that allows moving either the lens or the film in relation to the other. Eliminates or reduces the need for tilting the camera which would result in slanted lines. Helpful or necessary for architectural work.

Photomicroscopy: The technique of taking pictures through a microscope.

Plane of focus: The plane at which the lens is focused.

Proxar lens: Another name for a close-up lens that is mounted in front of the camera lens for photographing at closer distances.

Reflected meter: An exposure meter that measures the light reflected from the subject we are photographing. Exposure meters built into cameras are of the reflected type. The meter reading is affected by the brightness of the subject.

Retrofocus: A wide angle lens design with a very long back focus (distance from rear element to film plane) that is necessary on SLR cameras where the mirror needs the space to move up and down. Wide angle lenses on SLR cameras are of the retrofocus type. The other wide angle design, the optically true wide angle type, is used on large format and special medium format cameras.

Shutter: A device that is open a specific length of time to let light go to the image plane. The shutter can be in the camera, usually in front of the image plane (focal plane type) or in the lens.

Shutter speed: The length of time that the shutter in the camera or lens is open to let light travel to the image plane to make the exposure.

SLR camera: A camera type with a mirror that projects the image to the focusing screen for viewing. The mirror moves out of the way for taking the image. SLR (single lens reflex) cameras always show the image as it is recorded on the film. The image can also be viewed at the chosen aperture setting if the camera has a manual stop down control.

Spotmeter: An exposure meter that only measures a small area of the subject. A spotmeter can be built into the camera or be a separate accessory. The area that is measured is clearly indicated on the focusing screen in the camera or in the viewfinder of an accessory spotmeter.

Subject brightness: The amount of light that is reflected off a subject which must be considered when taking reflected exposure meter readings, also when using automatic or dedicated flash.

Teleconverter: A lens design that is used together with a camera lens to increase the focal length of the lens. The teleconverter is mounted between the camera and lens. A 2x converter doubles the focal length of the lens, a 1.4x converter lengthens the focal length 1.4x.

Telephoto lens: A lens that has a focal length longer than the standard (50mm for 35mm, 80mm for the 6x6 medium format). Telephoto lenses are usually separated into short telephotos going up to about double the focal length of the standard, and the longer types. A lens of the optically true telephoto design is physically shorter than its focal length. Most long camera lenses are of this design.

Transparency film: Records a positive image on the film, an image where the colors are the same as in reality, where black is recorded as black, and white as white. Such films are available for color and black and white photography.

Tripod: A camera accessory to support the camera for steadier operation than hand-held. Necessary or recommended with longer shutter speeds and/or longer focal length lenses.

TTL metering: TTL stands for "Through The Lens." It is usually used in connection with a light metering system that measures the light through the camera lens or a dedicated flash system that measures the flash reflected from the subject also through the lens.

Viewfinder: The camera component that is used to view the subject (an optical viewfinder) or lets you view the image of the subject on the focusing screen (as on a single reflex camera).

Wide angle distortion: Wide angle distortion refers to three dimensional subjects being recorded distorted (elongated) an the edges or corners of an image, especially when made with wide angle lenses on any camera. Mainly caused because the film plane is flat. Definitely not a fault in the wide angle lens design.

Wide angle lens: A lens with a focal length shorter than the standard. There are two optically different wide angle lens designs. An optically true wide angle design lens must be close to the film plane and can therefore not be used on SLR cameras. A retrofocus wide angle lens is necessary for this type of camera.

Zone system: A subject evaluation and metering system where the different subject brightness values from white to black are broken down into 10 zones. Black and white film developing times are adjusted to produce a black and white negative of normal contrast (printable on #2 paper), regardless what the contrast range of the original subject might have been.

Zoom effects: Produced by changing the focal length (zooming) while the image is recorded on the film. Zooming changes the image size while the subject or scene is recorded producing a streaking effect on the film.

Zoom lens: A lens design where the focal length can be changed within a certain range by moving some of the lens elements. The range of focal lengths is called the zoom range. True zoom lenses stay in focus when the focal length is changed, some require re-focusing.

Index

Other Books from Amherst Media, Inc.

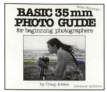

Basic 35mm Photo Guide
Craig Alesse

Great for beginning photographers! Designed to teach 35mm basics step-by-step — completely illustrated. Features the latest cameras. Includes: 35mm automatic and semi-automatic cameras, camera handling, *f*-stops, shutter speeds, and more! $12.95 list, 9x8, 112p, 178 photos, order no. 1051.

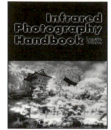

Infrared Photography Handbook
Laurie White

Covers black and white infrared photography: focus, lenses, film loading, film speed rating, heat sensitivity, batch testing, paper stocks, and filters. Black & white photos illustrate how IR film reacts in portrait, landscape, and architectural photography. $24.95 list, 8½x11, 104p, 50 b&w photos, charts & diagrams, order no. 1419.

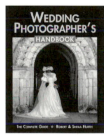

Wedding Photographer's Handbook
Robert and Sheila Hurth

The complete step-by-step guide: everything you need to start and succeed in the exciting and profitable world of wedding photography. Packed with shooting tips, equipment lists, must-get photos, business strategies, and much more! $24.95 list, 8½x11, 176p, index, b&w and color photos, diagrams, order no. 1485.

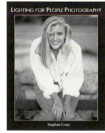

Lighting for People Photography
Stephen Crain

The complete guide to lighting and its different qualities. Includes: set-ups, equipment information, controlling strobe and natural lighting, and much more! Features diagrams, illustrations, and exercises for practicing the lighting techniques discussed in each chapter. $29.95 list, 8½x11, 112p, b&w and color photos, glossary, index, order no. 1296.

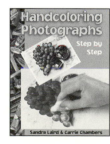

Handcoloring Photographs Step by Step
Sandra Laird & Carey Chambers

The new standard reference for handcoloring! Learn step-by-step how to use a wide variety of coloring media, such as oils, watercolors, pencils, dyes and tones, to handcolor black and white photos. Over 80 color photos illustrate how-to handcoloring techniques! $29.95 list, 8½x11, 112p, color and b&w photos, order no. 1543.

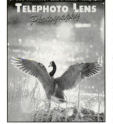

Telephoto Lens Photography
Rob Sheppard

A complete guide for telephoto lenses! This book shows you how to take great wildlife photos, portraits, sports and action shots, travel pics, and much more! Features over 100 photographic examples. $17.95 list, 8½x11, 112p, b&w and color photos, index, glossary, appendices, order no. 1606.

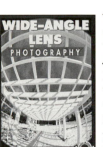

Wide-Angle Lens Photography
Joseph Paduano

For everyone with a wide-angle lens or people who want one! Includes taking exciting travel photos, creating wild special effects, using distortion for powerful images, and much more! Part of the Amherst Media's Photo-Imaging Series. $15.95 list, 7x10, 112p, glossary, index, appendices, b&w and color photos, order no. 1480.

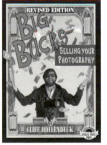

Great Travel Photography
Cliff and Nancy Hollenbeck

Learn how to capture great travel photos from the Travel Photographer of the Year! Includes helpful travel and safety tips, packing and equipment checklists, and much more! Packed full of photo examples for all over the world. Part of the Amherst Media's Photo-Imaging Series. $15.95 list, 7x10, 112p, b&w and color photos, index, glossary, appendices, order no. 1494.

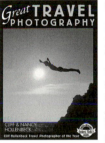

Big Bucks Selling Your Photography
Cliff Hollenbeck

A complete photo business package for all photographers. Includes secrets to making big bucks, starting up, getting paid the right price, and creating successful portfolios! Features setting financial, marketing and creative goals. This book helps to organize business planning, bookkeeping, and taxes. $15.95 list, 6x9, 336p, order no. 1177.

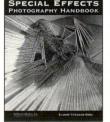

Special Effects Photography Handbook
Elinor Stecker Orel

Create magic on film with special effects! Little or no additional equipment required, use things you probably have around the house. Step-by-step instructions guide you through each effect. $29.95 list, 8½x11, 112p, 80+ color and b&w photos, index, glossary, order no. 1614.

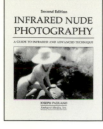

Infrared Nude Photography

Joseph Paduano

A stunning collection of images with informative how-to text. Over 50 infrared photos presented as a portfolio of classic nude work. Shot on location in natural settings, including the Grand Canyon, Bryce Canyon and the New Jersey Shore. $29.95 list, 8½x11, 96p, over 50 photos, order no. 1080.

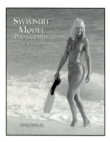

Glamour Nude Photography

Robert and Sheila Hurth

Create stunning nude images! Robert and Sheila Hurth guide you through selecting models, choosing locations, lighting, shooting techniques, posing, equipment, makeup, and much more! $24.95 list, 8½x11, 144p, over 100 b&w and color photos, index, order no. 1499.

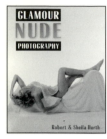

Swimsuit Model Photography

Cliff Hollenbeck

The complete guide to the business of swimsuit model photography. Includes: finding models, selecting equipment, posing, using props and backgrounds, and much more! $29.95 list, 8½x11, 112p, over 100 b&w and color photos, index, order no. 1605.

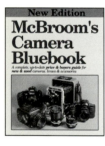

McBroom's Camera Bluebook

Mike McBroom

Comprehensive and fully illustrated, with price information on: 35mm cameras, medium & large format cameras, exposure meters, strobes and accessories. Pricing info based on equipment condition. A must for any camera buyer, dealer, or collector! $29.95 list, 8½x11, 224p, 75+ photos, order no. 1263.

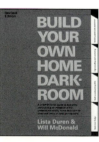

Build Your Own Home Darkroom

Lista Duren & Will McDonald

This classic book shows how to build a high quality, inexpensive darkroom in your basement, spare room, or almost anywhere. Information on: darkroom design, woodworking, tools, and more! $17.95 list, 8½x11, 160p, order no. 1092.

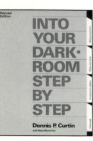

Into Your Darkroom Step-by-Step

Dennis P. Curtin

The ideal beginning darkroom guide. Easy to follow and fully illustrated each step of the way. Information on: equipment you'll need, set-up, making proof sheets and much more! $17.95 list, 8½x11, 90p, hundreds of photos, order no. 1093.

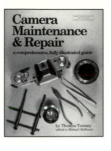

Camera Maintenance & Repair

Thomas Tomosy

A step-by-step, fully illustrated guide by a master camera repair technician. Sections include: testing camera functions, general maintenance, basic tools needed and where to get them, basic repairs for accessories, camera electronics, plus "quick tips" for maintenance and more! $24.95 list, 8½x11, 176p, order no. 1158.

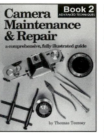

Camera Maintenance & Repair Book 2: Advanced Techniques

Thomas Tomosy

Building on the basics covered in the first book, this book will teach you advanced troubleshooting and repair techniques. It's easy to read and packed with photos. An excellent reference and companion book to *Camera Maintenance & Repair*! $29.95 list, 8½x11, 176p, order no. 1558.

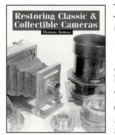

Restoring Classic & Collectible Cameras

Thomas Tomosy

A must for camera buffs and collectors! Clear, step-by-step instructions show how to restore a classic or vintage camera. Work on leather, brass and wood to completely restore your valuable collectibles. $34.95 list, 8½x11, 160p, b&w photos and illustrations, glossary, index, order no. 1613.

More Photo Books Are Available

Write or fax for a *FREE* catalog:
Amherst Media, Inc.
PO Box 586
Buffalo, NY 14226 USA

Fax: 716-874-4508

Ordering & Sales Information:

Individuals: If possible, purchase books from an Amherst Media retailer. Write to us for the dealer nearest you. To order direct, send a check or money order with a note listing the books you want and your shipping address. U.S. & overseas freight charges are $3.50 first book and $1.00 for each additional book. Visa and Master Card accepted. New York state residents add 8% sales tax.

Dealers, distributors & colleges: Write, call or fax to place orders. For price information, contact Amherst Media or an Amherst Media sales representative. Net 30 days.

All prices, publication dates, and specifications are subject to change without notice. Prices are in U.S. dollars. Payment in U.S. funds only.

CUT ALONG DOTTED LINE

Amherst Media's Customer Registration Form

Please fill out this sheet and send or fax to receive free information about future publications from Amherst Media.

CUSTOMER INFORMATION

DATE

NAME

STREET OR BOX #

CITY   STATE

ZIP CODE

PHONE ( )   FAX ( )

OPTIONAL INFORMATION

I BOUGHT *Achieving the Ultimate Image* BECAUSE

I FOUND THESE CHAPTERS TO BE MOST USEFUL

I PURCHASED THE BOOK FROM

CITY   STATE

I WOULD LIKE TO SEE MORE BOOKS ABOUT

I PURCHASE   BOOKS PER YEAR

ADDITIONAL COMMENTS

FAX to: 1-800-622-3298

IF MAILING, FOLD IN NUMBER ORDER ALONG DASHED LINES.

Name_____
Address_____
City_____State_____
Zip_____ — _____

Place
Postage
Here

Amherst Media, Inc.
PO Box 586
Buffalo, NY 14226

IF MAILING, PASTE UNDERSIDE OF FLAP, OR TAPE HERE.